JOURNEY THROUGH FEAR

by
Antoinette Lee Howard

For permission, or serialization, condensation, adaptions, or for our catalog of other publications, write to: Ozark Mountain Publishing, Inc., P.O. Box 754, Huntsville, AR 72740, Attn: Permissions Department.

Library of Congress Cataloging-in-Publication Data
Howard, Antoinette Lee - 1941 -
    "Journey Through Fear" by Antoinette Lee Howard
Understanding how judgment begins the process of fear in which we become imprisoned. Learn to exchange judgment for acceptance and you walk free.

1. Metaphysics 2. Fear 3. Channeling 4. Judgment
I. Howard, Antoinette Lee, 1941 -   II. Title

Library of Congress Catalog Control Number: 2009921266
ISBN: 978-1-886940-57-4

Cover Design: enki3d.com
Book Design: Julia Degan
Book Set in: Times New Roman

Published By

PO Box 754, Huntsville, AR 72740
800-935-0045 or 479-738-2348 fax: 479-738-2448

WWW.OZARKMT.COM
Printed in the United States of America

Many thanks to Marilyn, Lucy, Megan, and George for your belief and support, and to the devas for infinite patience.

The journey to love is indeed a journey through fear, because you must face all your fears as you make the decision to live in love.

Guardian of Communication

TABLE OF CONTENTS

PROLOGUE: VOICES   iii

SECTION I. EARTH'S ASTRAL CARETAKERS   1

1. Guardian of Water Clarification:
   Introducing the Devas   3
2. Merlin, Guardian of Communication:
   We Can Enter the Devic Realm   27

SECTION II. FEAR FILLS OUR LIVES   41

3. Judgment, the Entryway to Fear   43
4. Why We Choose to Live in Fear   67
5. Stopping Fear at Judgment   79

SECTION III.
THE CORE AND PRIMAL FEAR-PAIRS   91

6. The Core Fear-Pair of Powerlessness and Strength   93
7. The Core Fear-Pairs of Sickness and Health,
   Aging and Youth   109
8. The Core Fear-Pairs of Lack and Abundance,
   Failure and Success   131
9. The Primal Fears of Death and Life   151
10. Stopping Fear at the Core and Primal Fears   175

SECTION IV.
FEAR BEHAVIORS—AND ALTERNATIVES   181

11. Anger and Depression   183
12. Controller and Victim-Controller   197
13. The Whirlwind and Depletion   211
14. Sanctuary in the Past and the Future   225
15. Stopping Fear at the Fear Behaviors   237

EPILOGUE:
SETTING UP A CIRCLE OF HAPPINESS   243

ADDITIONAL READING   253

PROLOGUE
VOICES

We ask you to take a journey that requires as much
courage as a call to war, but it is courage of mind
rather than body.
We ask you to recognize that all of your battles, from the
fistfight on the school playground to the nuclear confrontation
that can obliterate all traces of life on the planet,
have their origins in fear. We ask you to journey past fear.

Guardian of Water Clarification

PROLOGUE: VOICES

We have watched you for many
eons, and have seen endless
changes in your garb and lore.
One thing has remained
consistent: You are a warlike
species. Heed our call to a way of
life that is different from yours,
with its emphasis on weaponry
and bravado.

Guardian of Water Clarification

I never planned to write about how you and I journey past fear.

On the cusp of the millennium, I was at a high and a low point: I was living my dream, but I was flying solo. At Christmastime several years earlier, my husband had been diagnosed with terminal cancer. One month after that grim news, as I stood in the mortuary chapel, staring at a white calla lily next to the small box that contained his ashes, I asked myself two obvious and long-overdue questions: How do I know I will be alive at this time next year? So, what am I doing with my life?

I knew I was a writer and painter at the age of eight, when I presented my illustrated poem, "Autumn Leaves, by Henrietta Thoreau," with a flourish to my grandmother. I had discovered *Walden* on her bookshelf that year. I did not understand some of the words and many of the concepts, but I knew I wanted a cabin in the woods, along with a generous supply of pencils and paper.

Sometime between that day and my sophomore year of college, though—I cannot quite pinpoint when—I gave up that dream for a practical career as a technical writer and illustrator. My husband, a photographer, had done the same type of thing, getting a "real job" as our daughter grew up, and doing the work he loved part-time.

We had made plans for a new start once she was on her own, but he would never have the chance. There had to be a way to make my part of that life we planned together—my old dream of nature writing and illustrating—work.

It took awhile to pay off the bills and land my first contract, but I left my job on a golden Indian Summer afternoon and started a series of illustrated articles on healing plants that evening. The work was not as poetic and inspiring as Henrietta's dream, and worries about depleting my small savings account nagged me, but it was a start.

A month later, I was seated at my drawing table in the studio/office/extra bedroom of my apartment, finishing the illustration for an article on the cold-fighting properties of *Echinacea purpurea*, the purple coneflower. Two studio lamps brought noon light to the room, even though it was close to midnight. My sleek black and white cat, Lucy, dozed in the warmth of the lamp next to my left elbow.

As I reached for a red pencil to heighten the rainbow of stained glass colors that surrounded the flower, I heard—or, more accurately, sensed—a flow of words. Intrigued, I reached for a drawing pad and turned to a blank page, as words flowed ahead of my pencil.

Change the focus. Indicate the veil of fog that nourishes me. Fog cloaks me in silence and sustenance, with the promise of sunlight. Place me in colors that are ripe with summer, yet touched with autumn.

I stared at the cat, who was snoring softly. "Everyone is a critic," I mumbled. She opened one green eye.

The sound of my words in the silent studio startled me into full awareness. I had worked late many nights before, but I had never heard *voices*. Then I stared at the illustration. Had I touched a new way of subconsciously analyzing my artwork?

But the words did not stop there.

> The Sun is my necessity, my powerhouse. I store its fire in my petals, seedhead, stem, leaves, and roots. I live by the green miracle of chlorophyll through the Sun's beneficence, filtered through Earth's gifts of water, air, and soil.

The Findhorn Garden, a book I had read in the mid-seventies, tugged at my memory. Peter and Eileen Caddy, along with Dorothy Maclean, had created a lush garden on the rugged, windswept northern Scotland coast with the help of devic guides. The word *deva* is a Sanskrit term that translates as *shining one*, and the primary role of these spirit guides is to harmonize the intricate dance of all life on Earth, including gardens such as Findhorn. Had I somehow attracted the attention of one of these nature guardians?

The whole idea was preposterous. I wrote in block letters: "THIS IS A FIRST—I AM TALKING TO MYSELF IN THE MIDDLE OF THE NIGHT!"

The words continued.

> Yes, you can call me a deva or a nature guardian. You can also call me an angel; I am in that lineage. Specifically, I am the guardian of the aster family. The flower *Echinacea*, which you draw and write about, is part of my watch.

One illustrated article for a regional magazine and the three- by ten-foot patch of strawberries and sunflowers outside my back door hardly put me in the company of the Caddys and Maclean. I wrote: "Why are you speaking to me?"

You think you have to be a master gardener to honor me, and through me, my children. I assure you it is not so. Soon I will be dead. My season, song, and fire will be complete. I will be reborn in your words and painting.

The message was confusing. Was I hearing the same voice? I jotted in the sketchbook: "Now you sound like the coneflower, not the deva."

I speak as the flower, to help you understand. I love humanity. I have consented to be a dooryard flower, living beside your homes. I am the bringer of health, and your ally against illness, as Earth leans farther from the Sun and darkness comes early. When my petals are downturned, as they are in your painting, you see a vessel that is satisfied and fulfilled. The seeds, the continuation of life, mature in my belly, open to the Sun.

I do not weep. I sing only of joy. My seedhead is full, and I live the life for which I was born. I am content to die with the coming of winter, knowing that my kin will bear new life in the spring. I will not see it, but I will be part of it, through my children and my roots in this place.

I stared at the pencil. Not only was this voice talking as if it—or she, or he—were the plant, it also was saying that the plant knew far more than I was comfortable thinking about.

I wrote: "You are telling me that the coneflower has chosen to cure our colds, that it has a sense of family, and that it knows about its death. That means the plant designs its life."

> My body pulses with green life, just as yours pulses with red life. Does it surprise you that I too can make choices, that I too can love? Expand your definition of *life*. Life—which can be defined as purpose and plan—exists in the electrons, protons, and neutrons of each atom, as well as in the dance of subatomic particles. And is not the atom the building block of *all* life, not just yours?
>
> You of red life consume our green life in our fullness. For the most part, you do so without gratitude or awareness. We of green life ask you to bow to our beauty and strength. Then we die with a sense of fulfillment.

My hand was shaking slightly. This voice was essentially saying that the flower—and extrapolating from there, all plants—appreciates our thanks. The words continued.

> Saying "thank you" is a powerful way to honor my kind, as well as all life.

While I was digesting the fact that plants were far more like people than I imagined, the point of view abruptly switched back to the devic voice.

> With neither green blood nor red, I stand beside your duality. Red life and green life are mirror images, and both must live in harmony to survive.

> I widen this discussion to emphasize that all expressions of life must live in union, and that all—everything you see, including your mother, the Earth—is alive. I ask you to be our intermediary, our voice to your kind.

I leaned so hard on the pencil that the point broke. I picked up another one, indigo this time, and stared at the casing, then at the sheet of paper. I wanted to paint and write about plants—but their *outsides*, not their green blood or their feelings. And what did the words "everything you see" mean? The voice answered my unspoken question.

> Everything has purpose and plan; that means everything is alive. Quantum physicists recognize the truth that thought influences the life inherent in the atom, and mystics already know. We add our voices to this still-soft chorus.
>
> Once you grasp the concept that all is alive and all is one, that union, not separation, is the baseline for life, you begin to live in harmony with your brothers and sisters, as well as with all life on Earth. Right now, humanity, buried in a sense of separateness and fear, literally holds the power to destroy the planet. It is why we speak to you, and why we ask you to speak to others of your kind—using your tools, writing and painting—about how to live.

The words stopped. I turned off the lights, carried the cat into the bedroom, and stared at the ceiling for the rest of the night. Given the outrageous concept that a deva was talking to me, exactly what did he—or she—expect? I was hardly an expert on the art of living expansively. My savings were close to nonexistent, and my client list consisted of one small, financially shaky magazine.

At five, I shuffled into the studio and reworked the illustration. By nine, I had e-mailed the illustrated article and was searching the library stacks. In addition to books I either had read or heard about—*The Findhorn Garden* and Peter Tompkins' *The Secret Life of Plants*—I discovered Eliot Cowan, a healer who works with plant mentors; Machaelle Small Wright, who created her lush Perelandra garden in Virginia with the help of devic guardians; Michael Roads, who met these guides near his Australian home and journeys into an ever-expanding reality; Marko Pogačnik, who contacts nature spirits in his work as a landscape healer; and Gwennie Armstrong Fraser, who began to sense devic presences in childhood.

There were two common threads in many of these books: a time of initial confusion, when the author worried about going crazy, and a decision to listen. I could relate to the going-crazy part. The real question was: Would I listen?

That evening, I thought about my options. The article I had mailed out was not precisely what eight-year-old Henrietta Thoreau had dreamed of writing, but it was a big step away from computer manuals and grant proposals. Did I really want to commit the time to transcribe these communications, and would I ever find a publisher? In addition—I hummed the theme of Rod Serling's *Twilight Zone*—did I want to be known as the woman who talks with spirits? That one was the clincher: I would stay with what I knew.

As I began to turn off the lamps, I sensed another voice. My decision wavered, as words that I had copied from Fraser's introduction to *The Golden Web* taunted me from my drawing pad: "The Devas' communications represent a distillation of the consciousness within Nature and of the patterns of life that shape physical matter and the world we inhabit. In their communications, the Devas call us to develop a much deeper awareness of Nature, of its profound beauty, intricacy and sensitivity, and to recognise and respect the life we share."*

Was I *really* going to ignore the voices?

I pulled out a pencil—olive green this time—and turned to a blank page in my sketchbook. I gave myself one last out: The minute I got bored or scared, I would forget the whole thing.

In the hundreds of communications that I have received since that November night, boredom has never been a problem. And, although a number of messages are frightening, in that they deal with the potential fate of humanity in uncompromisingly blunt terms, I have sensed nothing but kindness and love behind the words, and one overriding goal: to help us live free from fear. On the other hand, issues that I did not care to think about personally, culminating with the fears of death, sickness, and age that permeate the human race, have been as hard to face as a Tyrannosaurus Rex.

Words tumbled ahead of my pencil.

You can be gods but you are children.

I was only marginally committed to this work, and now a voice was portraying me, along with the rest of humanity, in a less than flattering light. At the same time, though, I was intrigued. I wrote: "Why do you call us children?"

When you live in fear, you are a child, whatever your age. I illustrate the concepts of childhood and adulthood in terms of your life story. You think of your role as that of a writer and painter, with nature your subject. I tell you that nature at its highest, the saving of the planet, is your focus. To that end, you need to examine

---

* Gwennie Armstrong Fraser, The Golden Web: A New Partnership with Nature (Findhorn, Scotland: Findhorn Press, 1995), 10.

separateness and fear, which keep you children, and union and acceptance, which bring you to harmony within yourself, and beyond, with all life. Only then do you begin to approach real adulthood. Only then do you begin to save the Earth.

I understood the logic—if you could call it that—behind the first communication. As I was painting the coneflower, its devic guardian spoke. Did this brusque voice belong to the same deva? I did not need to write the question.

I am the Guardian of Water Clarification. I watch the flow of water back to the great underground reservoirs. We will speak of my work, as well as the work of other guardians, in depth.

You must understand that this is a time of travail, and that only love will save your kind, as well as the Earth. Do you agree to do your part?

I stared at my drawing book, my pencil, the lamps, the cat. This was work that Henry David Thoreau—or at least my grandmother—would have agreed to do, I was sure of it. I nodded.

THE GOAL OF *JOURNEY THROUGH FEAR*

The purpose of this book is to help you break your addiction to fear. If you are like most of us, if you judge what happens to you individually, as well as what takes place in your family, community, nation, and the world, as bad or good, wrong or right, it is you whom the devas address.

In effect, once you make a judgment, you enter your personal version of solitary confinement. You do not need cement-block walls and a distant, barred view of the sky to be imprisoned in fear. The book is titled *Journey Through Fear* because, for most of us, our baseline is fear, and judgment is where we begin.

Once you judge a situation or issue—and the person behind it—as bad or good, wrong or right, you feel separate from the person you blame, and ultimately from all life. This sense of isolation contaminates you with fear, up to and including the fear of death and life. You then act out your fear through fear behaviors, which affect you and infect others.

It is not until you exchange judgment for acceptance, which gives freedom to the situation or issue, as well as the players involved, to resolve in the best way, that you walk free. You acknowledge, "I see my part in this drama, but not the whole," which is humbling, but always true. You are able to accept all, because you see yourself in all whom you would judge.

The potential inherent in acceptance, rather than judgment, is vast. Once enough of us change our thoughts, society begins to change. Your and my journey through fear contains the promise of Utopia.

HOW THE BOOK IS ORGANIZED

Two speakers emerged once I agreed to write about this journey through and past fear: the Guardian of Water Clarification, who spoke that second night; and Merlin, the famous shaman and advisor to King Arthur, now the Guardian of Communication. You will hear their stories in the first section, and their voices continue throughout the book.

My devic guides have always known exactly where I was in the writing—and, most important, the thinking—process. I received a number of communications on the topic of judgment, for example, until I finally grasped it. I have winnowed out the repetition, to give you the heart of their message. When I asked if this type of editing was acceptable, their unequivocal answer was that this is my book. They offered no guidance on how it should be written or organized, assuming that once I understood the concepts, I would be able to communicate them to you. I add that if you find any mistakes, they have nothing to do with the devas, but with my comprehension.

In Section I, *Earth's Astral Caretakers*, the Guardian of Water Clarification discusses how devas are born and how they live. Ultimately, the devic plane is open to all. Merlin decided to make this transition while he was still alive; in fact, he created his post as the Guardian of Communication.

Section II, *Fear Fills Our Lives*, describes how judgment leads us into fear, how all-pervasive fear is, and why we choose to live in fear. Fear offers us enticing gifts, including the sense of being alive and safe. The section ends with guidelines for stopping fear in its tracks at the point of judgment.

Section III, *The Core and Primal Fear-Pairs*, examines what happens after we judge a situation or an issue, as well as the person behind it, as bad or good, wrong or right. At this point, we experience fear in its various disguises: fear of our powerlessness as well as our strength; fear of sickness and health, along with age and youth; and fear of lack and abundance, plus failure and success. We also confront our primal fears of death and life. The section concludes with a chapter on how to neutralize the fear-pairs before they escalate into fear behaviors.

Section IV, *Fear Behaviors—and Alternatives*, describes our primary coping mechanisms when we are filled with fear. We lash out at ourselves and others through anger; attempt to control others, both directly and as victims; bury ourselves in a whirlwind of activity that leaves us too numb to think, and then feel depleted; or retreat to the past and the future, so we do not have to face the present. When we are the midst of acting out fear through these behaviors, we most often consider ourselves justified and in charge of our lives. The section ends with a chapter on how to identify and eliminate these destructive actions.

Note the use of the word *and* in these pairs of seeming opposites. If you are angry with another, you also are angry with yourself, or depressed; if you try to control others, you also feel like a victim; if you obsess about death, you also fear life; and so forth.

In the chapters concerned with identifying and dealing with judgment, the major fears, and the fear behaviors, you will find a series of questions. As I grappled with my personal journey through fear, the devas asked me some thought-provoking questions. In turn, I pass them along to you.

In the Epilogue, the Guardian of Water Clarification discusses how we create a circle of happiness. In healing ourselves, we do our part to heal the planet. In fact, once one-tenth of humanity chooses to leave fear behind, we can make the transition from the darkness of dissension, destruction, and war to the light of peace.

FEAR BEHAVIORS

*Your actions toward others
and self arise directly from fear*

Anger ~
Depression

Controller ~
Victim-Controller

FEAR

*Once you make a judgment,
you enter the realm of fear*

Whirlwind ~
Depletion

Retreat to
Past ~ Future

Life ~ Death

Powerlessness ~ Strength

Sickness ~
Health

Aging ~
Youth

Failure ~
Success

Lack ~
Abundance

JUDGMENT

*The seed thought
behind all fear*

Good ~ Bad

Right ~ Wrong

THE THREE STAGES OF FEAR

SECTION I
EARTH'S ASTRAL CARETAKERS

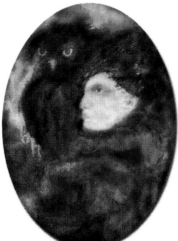

Guardian of Communication

As your mind frees itself from
fear, it fills with light and
becomes transparent, much
like a leaded glass window with
bright sun streaming through it.
When your mind is filled with
fear, it is dark and opaque, much
like a smoke-damaged window
in a burnt-out building.

Humans are capable of the
atrocities of Attila the Hun
as well as the holiness of
Jesus of Nazareth.
That is why we describe you
as warriors as well as kings.

Guardian of Water Clarification

Chapter One

GUARDIAN OF
WATER CLARIFICATION:
INTRODUCING THE DEVAS

We are minds too, in different
garb, with different jobs. We
work on the astral plane, which
gives birth to the physical.

Guardian of Water Clarification

We live in physical bodies; devas are, in essence, condensed thought. They are born of the coalesced thought of their kind, they communicate with one another through vision powered by thought, and they harmonize all life on Earth, from its fiery core to the farthest reaches of the atmosphere, through thought-pictures.

They temper this immense power of thought with an equal measure of love. Without this component of love—in other words, at our level of fear—they could destroy the Earth. One angry thought on the part of the devic guardian of the Gulf Stream could alter its course and create frigid wastelands in temperate regions; one despairing thought on the part of the devic guardian of the grasses that strengthen the soil could result in a worldwide Dust Bowl. Although catastrophes can and do occur as the Earth readjusts to changing conditions, the devas' vision of harmony helps the planet to regulate and heal itself. Without devic guardians, you would not be reading these words and I would not be writing them.

I spent quiet nighttime hours trying to envision a world filled with the kind of love that the devas exemplify, and could not manage it. At the same time, I knew that saints, from Francis of Assisi to modern-day masters such as Mother Theresa and my yogic guru, Paramahansa Yogananda, had crossed that huge divide. Could we all really do so? And what of the devas? Had they been saints before they died?

The Guardian of Water Clarification patiently answered my questions, and added some mind-blowing concepts to the mix.

* * *

The Guardian of *Echinacea* said that you are in the same category as angels. Most religious literature defines angels as a special creation of God.

> Devas and angels were not created separately, nor are we separate from one another or from you. Consider us your older siblings, and you are close to the truth of our relationship. Once you learn to live in love, the devic, or angelic, state is open to everyone.
>
> Understand that we use words as pointers, to clarify your awareness. In these communications, we use commonly accepted terminology. Thus, the term *deva* signifies one who works with natural forces and life on Earth; *angel* describes a guardian spirit for humanity, either individually—what you call guardian angels—or by belief system, race, or other divisions; and *nature spirit* denotes a guardian for individuals or groups in the animal, mineral, and plant kingdoms. In reality, there is no such

division. Using these definitions, the Guardian of Communication, with whom you will speak in depth, and I could be considered angels, because we are working with you. However, we use the term *deva* to underscore the fact that we broaden our focus to all life forms, not specifically humanity.

We live a single truth: All Is One. I watch water; the Guardian of Communication sings harmony for the spoken and written word; other guardians watch great landmasses and air currents; and still others sing harmony for individuals such as you. None of us is greater or lesser than another, and each knows the whole, be it your need for a specific word or the Equator's need for trees to regulate the planetary heat circulation.

EVERY ATOM IS A MIND

The implications of All Is One are immense. Practically applied, it means that the guardian of the one-day-old baby and the watcher of the Himalayas have the same purpose: to assist the form that is in their care to achieve a state of harmony with the conditions in which it lives, and with all life on Earth. That state of harmony, or union, is an expression of love.

You are saying that there is no difference between a mountain range and a person.

That is correct. Keep in mind what the Guardian of *Echinacea* said: The atom is alive, and it serves as the building-block for all life. We bless all forms in which atomic life manifests: animal, mineral, and plant. It is hard to see the interconnectedness of life, particularly in this era, when you worship your belief in what your senses experience, as translated by the brain. In time, you must access wisdom. You can do that only when you embrace mind, which unites sense data that is translated by the brain with the Infinite Intelligence that lies behind all life. It is your ultimate goal.

Is mind, as you define it, what is known as the soul; and is Infinite Intelligence another name for God?

Yes. Mind, or soul, is your connection with this overriding intelligence in creation, or God. We use the term *mind* because it is less emotionally burdened than the word *soul*.

As an expression of life, each atom can be considered a mind. (There are layers of mind smaller than the atom, but we use that as a baseline for this discussion.) In truth, you are not an individual; you are an aggregate of atoms, a group of minds that has elected to coalesce in human form to learn lessons about awareness and union, under the direction of a primary mind. Every plant, mineral deposit, and animal, from the microscopic to the largest that you can imagine, has a primary, or directing, mind. It has made the leap from the group mind of the atom, which agrees to be part of a larger form, to a dream of individual expression. An atom in your fingertip, in your jade necklace, or in the philodendron on the nearby table may decide to incarnate as a Buddha, based on its experience in your form or in your presence. At a certain point of development, all atoms choose to incarnate as primary minds.

You are talking about unimaginable numbers of primary minds and forms. The Earth would be inundated.

Expand your vision beyond your home planet. In the Milky Way alone, there are innumerable planetary environments. Additionally, a primary mind may choose to live in a completely different milieu, such as your Sun or an asteroid. To keep this discussion within bounds, we limit it to life on Earth, but life as an entirety is much vaster than you imagine.

I assume that the forms you mentioned—jade, the philodendron, the Sun, and an asteroid—have primary minds. My cat, Lucy, has one too.

That is correct.

Do water, air, and soil have primary minds?

Yes. It is hard to envision the primary, or directing, mind behind the Gulf Stream, the Mississippi Delta, the Jet Stream, or even the Earth's core, but one exists. Just as your mind harmonizes the work of each atom in your body, from conception to death, so do these primary minds make contact with each atom within their purview.

In addition, just as your mind directs the brain, which, when used fully, mediates between the outer world of the senses and the Universal

Intelligence, so also do these magnificent primary minds coalesce their outer and inner worlds. In the Gulf Stream, for example, the primary mind calls on the sense impressions of dolphins and whales in the way that you rely on your senses.

Ultimately, All Is One. Your mind is one with the primary and atomic minds of philodendron, cat, Gulf Stream, Earth, Sun, and Universal Intelligence, or God.

THE DEVIC PLANE IS OPEN TO ALL

Given All Is One, then you also are a primary mind.

Yes. We are primary minds that no longer need to join with atomic minds in form. We are of the ether, the dark matter that fills the universe. That is our birthplace, if you will.

Are you a man or a woman?

Just as we have no form as you know it, gender is also not an issue. Speak of me as he or she; in fact, it may be best to interchange these references.

How old are you?

Old is a relative term. By whose standards do you define age? In our realm, I am younger than many. In your years, I predate the pyramids.

Are you conceived and born in the same way as human babies?

We are not born as babies are to your kind, but as unformed spirits. Energy contained in an oval—an egg—of mist is coalesced from the thoughts of our kind, a mind is attracted to that energy, and a new devic spirit appears. Any mind can choose to be born in the devic plane, if it has progressed to the point at which it no longer lives in fear. If a mind still has fear to eradicate, it is not aware of the devic dimension as an option. It goes on to other embodiments—other forms—on the physical plane.

You are searching for commonalities in your life and ours. I—either as an atomic group mind or as a primary mind—have experienced the life dance in all forms of matter: animal, vegetable, and mineral; land, water, and air, starting with the Big Bang. So have you. While I was incarnated, I learned to live in total acceptance and union with the whole fabric of life—what you term love. So can you. That is the purpose of these discussions.

Could I make a choice to be a deva in this lifetime—given, of course, that I learn to live in love?

Yes. A few minds do elect to make the transition to the devic state while they are still in human—or animal, mineral, plant, air, water, or soil—form. The Guardian of Communication made this decision while he was embodied as Merlin; you will hear more about that choice from him. On the other hand, I, along with most, chose the devic dimension following my death as a shaman.

THE CYCLE OF REINCARNATION

In light of this discussion, obviously we do not "go to heaven" after we die.

> After death, the primary mind—what you consider *you*—travels to the astral dimension, which can be considered heaven, because you are open to the blissful, omnipresent love of God. However, you do not stay there. Contrary to the philosophy behind much religious thought, you make the decision to reincarnate until you complete your journey through fear to love.
>
> I add that God does not judge you; you judge yourself. And I assure you that after death, your primary mind, without the cloak of reason and the senses, is totally honest.

Do all atoms make this transition too?

> Yes. They evaluate their sojourns in form, and make decisions accordingly. Since atomic minds exist as part of a form, they do not judge the form's evolution the way the primary mind does. They do, however, evaluate what they need to experience, and choose anew. If an atom feels that it understands all forms of life—animal, vegetable, mineral, air, water, soil—it elects to become a primary mind. That is its next logical step.
>
> As we continue this discussion, we will use the word *mind* to indicate the primary rather than the atomic mind, the mind that you consider *you*.

What if I am an atheist and believe that life is all there is? Or what if I do not believe in reincarnation? Our expectations and beliefs must color the way we experience death.

> No. After death, you may sleep for a while, until you can accept the reality of the astral world, but you inevitably learn the truth. There are spirits who work with such minds.

Why don't we remember our former lives, right back to the Big Bang?

> Babies are born remembering the love of God that pervades the astral world, along with former lives, but by the age of three or four, they close to that truth. For example, at the age of two, you were aware of your lives as a poet in India and a doctor in New England, lives you have long since forgotten.
>
> The primary reason for this shuttering of consciousness is that you become engrossed in life on this plane, and it appears to be the only reality. However, there can be a myriad number of other explanations. You may live with others who fear the paranormal, and take on their fears; you may accept a faith that teaches that belief in reincarnation is sinful; or you may decide that only what you can contact with your senses is real, and reject the concept of an afterlife. Additionally, you may simply choose to forget. If you remembered all the lives that you have led, with a liberal dose of malice in many of them, you could believe it impossible to strive for perfection in this life.

I add that once you become free of fear, once you live in the state of love, you remember all of your lives and are aware of the astral realm. A growing number of people have that level of understanding, and it can be yours.

Tell me more about what happens after death.

You review all of your incarnations, along with why you chose them, and then plan your next lifetime. Your time in the astral dimension is devoted to this type of reflection. You are in the presence of the all-encompassing love of God, and you desire to retain that level of love forever. Believe me, you *strive* to perfect yourself as you chart your next life.

I say this about those who have lived ethical lives. For those who have chosen darkness—despots, mass murderers, and the like—the time after death is devoted to sleep and healing. When the mind awakens, it is ready to plan a new life. Often it chooses a meditative state in the mineral or plant kingdom, not necessarily a human existence, in order to cleanse its former tendencies.

Keep in mind that all minds are equal. What matters is the mind's development, not the physical form that it assumes. All minds—both atomic minds and primary minds—experience all major types of existence, in order to evolve into fullness of being. Your incarnations as a primary mind on Earth, for example, include cheetah, rose, and marble, as well as human. Additionally, as algae and lichen, you have been part of the water and the air, as well as the soil.

WE ARE BORN TO FULFILL OUR LIFE PURPOSES AND GOALS

Is there any standard sequence that an atomic mind takes, once it decides to become a primary mind?

There is no specified order—a mind chooses what it needs—but the usual progression is from mineral to plant to animal, including expressions as a human.

Is the human form the highest state?

Minerals and plants are primarily thought-directed, and animals are primarily action-oriented, but the mind's goal in all states is to combine thought with action. For the plant and mineral, movement is secondary to thought; and for the animal, with the exception of the human, thought is secondary to activity. In the human form, you have the opportunity to combine both thought and action fully, so in that sense it is the highest state.

I do not understand the concept of action. A cheetah takes care of its young and seeks food, but what does a rose or a piece of marble do?

As a rose, thought directs your growth and your work to produce young. As part of the structure of marble, your thought helps to arrange minerals into the form marble. Although thought directed to form may not seem like action as you understand the word, it is precisely that.

What you are describing sounds like instinct, rather than thought.

We differentiate thought, which implies the power of reason and choice, from instinct, which is an inborn pattern of behavior. All life forms, including humans, inherit some behavior patterns: the drive to procreate your kind, for example. Assume that if you can go past this instinctual drive through choice and reason, though, so can all other life forms. Scientists are beginning to touch this fundamental truth in the world of subatomic particles, which choose their state of existence as particle or wave. By comparison with a quark, a rose bush or a piece of marble is vast.

The concepts of thought and action bring us to life purposes and goals. Each life form—each primary mind—chooses life purposes that strengthen it individually and help sustain its kind. It also has a goal in relation to other life on Earth.

The life purposes of the rose are to bear young and to feed insects and birds, in order to ensure the continuation of its kind. In this case, its life purposes become one with its goal, which is to harmonize plant and animal interactions. Similarly, the life purposes of marble are to strengthen the deposit as a whole, and to interact with other mineral and plant forms to assure optimum conditions for all. Again, its life purposes harmonize with its goal of helping to neutralize stresses in the land around it. Marble and rose are powerful integrators of life, and you learned much about the concept of All Is One in those incarnations.

A cheetah has a goal too, beyond its life purposes of rearing its young and finding new territory for its kind. Along with other predatory cats, it streamlines the herbivore population. In effect, the predators ensure that herbivores are healthier, more able to cope with their environment. You learned to streamline your life and to go forward with strong intention in that incarnation.

What are humanity's life purposes and overall goal?

Similarly to the cheetah and the rose, humans bear and rear young to continue the species. Additionally, each person adopts one or more roles, or professions, that are not only personally fulfilling, but also help the larger family of humanity.

The term *life purpose*, as it will be used from now on, refers to this work. The diversity of these roles—architect, cook, counselor, businessperson, minister, homemaker, musician, lawyer, doctor, sculptor, police officer, politician, to name but a few—marks humans as different from other species. Through thought, combined with action, humans open choices for themselves that other species lack.

In concert with all other life, the goal of humanity is to expand beyond the small boundaries marked *self, family,* and *societal affiliation* to live as the great masters of every faith do, in a state of expanded love that sees all life as equal, interrelated, and sacred, from the amoeba to the planet itself.

The Biblical admonition that places humanity in a position of supremacy over all life has been translated incorrectly; the word *dominion* is interpreted most accurately as *stewardship*. Each person's goal is to act as a guardian for the other life forms that share the planet. This, in fact, is the reason that you experience all life forms, both as an atomic mind and a primary mind; it is the only way to live as one with all life.

This sense of oneness, or union, contrasts with fear, which concentrates on the individual, and gives rise to a sense of separation. It is easiest as well as hardest to achieve a sense of union as a human, because you have a wider sphere of awareness and many more options than other forms of life. Humans are capable of the atrocities of Attila the Hun and the holiness of Jesus of Nazareth.

You said you made the choice to become a deva after you died as a shaman. What other forms of life did you experience?

My incarnations on Earth included marble—I knew you in that state—as well as oak, coyote, and shaman. Because I had conquered fear, the devic realm was open to me after I died as a spirit healer in what is present-day Chile.

DEVIC WORK

Tell me about your work.

As a newborn devic spirit, I was visualized for a particular path: to assist eleven others who oversee the flow of water from the Earth's surface to the great underground rivers and reservoirs, which purify it. However, we have free will, just as you do. I traveled many byways before I took my place. For thousands of years, I trod your roads. I enjoyed concerts at Versailles, as well as the drumming of aborigines. I particularly liked Mozart; he was vitally alive and passionate. I am still a devotee of opera, concerts, and plays—and I never have to pay admission! Among others, I have seen Aeschylus, Shakespeare, Wagner, and Lloyd-Weber.

It sounds as if you should be a muse of the arts.

I could have chosen to be such a guardian. The decision was mine. I recognized that the truth of my core being—the perfection of water—is exactly what all creative minds do: purify, reduce to essentials, and make whole. I selected the work that I was born to do, because it is my best path.

Once you begin your work as a deva, do you continue it until the end of time?

We are always free to choose another existence. There are many options available on the astral level. We can decide to become guardians of another type of life on Earth, select another star system or galaxy, or choose another universe. Once you pass the barrier created by fear, you can explore many pathways to help other life evolve. You become a caretaker, a guardian.

How do you purify water?

I do not distil and filter water *per se*; that is the Earth's job. My work is to oversee the flow of water from the surface to its underground purification sources. There are many ways that water flow can be impeded as the Earth's crust adjusts to internal and external pressures, from changes at the core to the planet's movement through the fabric of space. The crust is constantly moving, although you are not always aware of these adjustments.

My job, if you will, is to provide a blueprint for the most efficient flow of the primary mind that you call water. Just as you do not build a home without some sort of plan, so also the water can call for a design that meets changing conditions, in order to assist its flow through rock to the aquifers, or to create new reservoirs, if necessary. This communication is not through words, but thought-pictures of the most efficient flow pattern.

I add that water can decide not to follow a particular thought-picture. Just as you have the freedom to become Attila or Jesus, so the water has freedom to make decisions regarding flow.

Tell me more about these thought-pictures.

Every deva is a guardian of the basic law, a keeper of a library, if you will. I use water that you can visualize, the Gulf Stream, as an example. It is fluid, and, as such, can move in wide arcs. The guardian projects thought-pictures of its optimum flow, as well as a sense of stability, to the primary mind. Note that I do not say that the Guardian of the Gulf Stream *forces* it to its path. If it changes course in reaction to stress, the guardian's vision helps it to return to harmony.

Why would water decide not to follow the blueprint?

The immense flows of air and water that blanket the Earth react to stress. For example, in your home in the Southwest, development pressures are reducing the movement of water back to the aquifers, and the water resources are increasingly strained. The water flow is changing because of these pressures.

Will we run out of water?

When great flows readjust, many other issues develop, including modifications to the rainfall cycle. I do not like to predict outcomes, because they can change. Once you begin to live less fearfully, once you begin to conserve and honor water, it can heal.

But you do know what will happen if we do nothing.

If you do nothing, you will experience searing temperatures and droughts to add to the strain of depleted water. Of course, this is not only true of your region; water resources throughout the world are experiencing the same types of pressures.

How does water make the kinds of decisions that you are talking about? How does it modify your thought-pictures?

It is not a decision as you think of the term, just as pulling your hand away from a hot stove is not a decision as much as it is a reaction. Water, air, and soil all react to stress caused by change. In the case of water, the normal flow to the aquifers may be so drastically reduced that some of the channels may dry up. In response, the water may divert to an aboveground route, rather than percolating into the ground. In that scenario, much water would be lost to evaporation, further depleting the supply.

We are discussing water, but Earth's three vast systems of air, water, and soil are intimately related, and stress in one impacts the others. Other parts of your nation and the world will experience earthquakes as the Earth's rock skeleton adjusts in response to reduced water flow, and still other areas will experience hurricanes, tornadoes, and other air-related adjustments. The planet is a giant living organism. Until you treat it as such, you run great risk, to yourselves and to all life on Earth.

If you saw the planet dying, would you do something to save it?

We work to save it every day with our songs of harmony. Remember, we act on the astral plane, not the physical, so do not expect us to avert wars or nullify the effects of global warming. If human beings choose to override planetary harmony, rather than work with us to enhance it, they have the freedom to do so. However, without humanity's cooperation and at the current level of destruction, most life as you know it will be gone within one hundred years. This includes humankind.

Will the Earth survive?

The planet has endured many such upheavals, including advanced civilizations—as sophisticated as yours—that have destroyed themselves. This is the first time that the challenge is planetary, however, rather than limited to one geographic area. In response to this level of stress, the planet may well slough off all life. Other planets have done so.

Are there practical things we can do as individuals?

By all means, practice sound conservation practices and support groups that would legislate changes in how humanity treats the natural world. Most importantly, though, change your thought pattern from separation, which is born of fear, to union with your brothers and sisters, as well as all life.

The saying, "thoughts are things," is literally true. You have read about miracles of bodily healing that take place when people let go of fear. The planet can heal in the same way. Fear—which the great systems of soil, water, and air translate into stress—is the ultimate destroyer.

Tell me about the work of other devic guardians.

In my realm of water, other guardians watch bodies of water, from lakes to oceans, and harmonize the flow of streams, rivers, and ocean currents. Some of this work overlaps; for example, the Guardian of the Atlantic and the Guardian of the Gulf Stream work in tandem.

Additionally, devic guardians sing harmony for air flows such as the Jet Stream, as well as the global blanket of air. They also oversee the changes of the seasons, and the surge of rock from Earth's fiery core to the surface. They look after vast areas of land on Earth, as well as the lunar surface.

Still other devas watch over plant and animal families, as well as mineral deposits. Using thought-pictures, what we term *shared vision*, these guardians bring species of plants and animals, as well as rocks and elements, into being. They then care for them throughout their life cycles.

I add that our love encompasses all. I watch water, but I bless all life. I have a focus, but I am larger than that area of concentration, just as there is more to you than your focus, which is writing and painting. We live the truth: All Is One.

You say devas create new life. How is that done?

The Universal Intelligence created the wisdom within the Earth for new life, and we work with that wisdom. To do so, we each adjust a picture, an ideal of perfection, until it resonates.

I use the jack in the pulpit, a wildflower that grows in moist, wooded areas and one of your favorites, as an example. First, the devic guardian of the *Arum* family visualized its form: the forward bend of its protective hood over the spadix, the stripes inside the hood, and the arrangement of its leaves. The guardian then pictured its place in the landscape, its season of bloom, its life purposes and goal, and its relationships with the astral as well as the physical world. Before it was placed in the landscape, all devic guardians and nature spirits saw, and added to, its beauty and form. This combined energy resulted in a flower of elegance and perfection, as well as rightness of place.

The jack in the pulpit, then, was literally a vision that was breathed into life at the moment of its completion by the strength of our collective dream. At that point, the guardian began to watch the form, by providing thought-pictures, as I described earlier.

Where do guardian angels and nature spirits fit into this picture?

Guardian angels, or nature spirits, are caretakers of individuals. Each jack in the pulpit has a nature spirit as a guardian, as do you. You will not meet nature spirits at this time. Because your emphasis is the big picture as you chart your passageway through fear, it is appropriate that devic guardians speak.

Again, I emphasize that we use terms such as *devic guardian, guardian angel, nature spirit,* and *angel* to make our foci clearer to you, but you must understand that lines of demarcation are not stratified in our realm. We live in oneness. When I say that there are no distinctions, that statement includes the Universal Intelligence, or God, as your—and my—most loving friend and equal.

You bring harmony to these words as you translate them for your brothers and sisters, I sing harmony for water, and God sings harmony for countless universes.

Ha! Now you are wondering if devic guardians have more clout than nature spirits as we create new forms. I remind you that bureaucracy is a human invention.

I do not speak to discomfit you, but to remind you to broaden your focus. It is hard to leave your culture and time. We will say many things that will expand your boundaries.

SHARED VISION: THE BASIS OF DEVIC COMMUNICATION

In addition, I respond to your thoughts to remind you of an important concept: You can access shared vision, or thought-pictures, right now, when you are a clear enough channel. That is why you intuit sickness among family members and friends, for example, and why you can hear us. These nonverbal expressions will become the standard means of communication among your kind in the not-so-distant future. What is now e-mail will become mind-mail, using shared vision.

Describe shared vision.

To use your terms and technology, shared vision combines time-lapse photography, which condenses a life cycle into a matter of seconds, with holography, which shows a form in three dimensions. Add to this the ability to broadcast these pictures to all in the devic realm instantaneously, and you have our concept of shared vision.

We communicate with you in the same way; however, your mind, rooted in your time and place, limits how you receive our messages. You sense ideas, which you translate into words, because words represent communication as you know it.

Consider the fact that many of your problems deal with words, which trail confusion the way a jet plane traces a contrail in the ocean of air. Like chameleons, words wear many colors of meaning. In addition, you have as many languages and grammars as you have countries. In contrast, shared vision allows us to see the totality, the full life cycle of an object. There is no lag time and no chance to misunderstand, both of which are essential when we create new life.

Once you make the decision to access shared vision, you—and all of humanity—can communicate that way. It is part of your genetic and mental blueprint, if you will; you simply have not yet made the choice to do it.

Why do we back off from it?

When you accept shared vision, you also accept that your thoughts will be transparent to everyone else, as well as to all life. Are you willing to make that leap?

That is a huge step. We would have to think differently.

That is the goal of these communications, to help you think differently. When love is your

driver rather than fear, this type of communication
will become commonplace.

Chapter Two

MERLIN, GUARDIAN OF COMMUNICATION: WE CAN ENTER THE DEVIC REALM

Speak your truth, clearly, without
fear, and you are free. Hide it,
and you are a slave.

Guardian of Communication

A shaman and guide to King Arthur, Merlin lived from the sixth century through the Renaissance, and could still be alive if he so chose. He made the conscious choice to die after deciding to serve as the Guardian of Communication.

* * *

I live in windswept caves on high hills, in mossy caves below the great ice fields, in river caves far beneath the breath of winter. I am Merlin.

The Merlin? The magician in T. H. White's *The Once and Future King*?

Yes. Tell people that their magician is now minding their words. Call me the patron saint of words, opening you and others to your core knowledge, your truth. Be it fiction or nonfiction, truth is your goal.

If I were able to give you just one piece of advice, it would be to smile, because you find your truth in joy, not fear. Caves and crystals are my stock-in-trade, but I trust that I do not disappoint your sense of my exalted purpose when I tell you that sometimes I join the revelers at a back-slapping football game, viewed on a large screen in a smoke-filled bar.

Your laughter is contagious. If you smiled at all in life, what a joyous, peaceful time all would have, as people and nations relaxed. It is so easy and so near. I want to shake your earnest shoulders and tell you to be happy every day.

It is not always easy to be happy. Countries are at war, and too often communities and families become emotional battlegrounds. Plus loved ones—and we—get sick and die.

Smile even when you are fearful or angry, sick or sad. The mind relies on the physical senses; the body, in effect, has wisdom that the mind taps. Your smile tells your mind that all is well in your immediate surroundings, that your senses detect no danger lurking inside or outside your body at this moment.

Most importantly, your smile reassures your mind that it is possible to live in peace. Even if you are in the midst of dealing with sickness or death, even if you are part of an emotional or physical combat zone, there is something small or large to smile about every day: a friend's kindness, a bird outside your window, a dandelion with the audacity to grow in a bluegrass lawn, a poem, a delicious meal, your own courage in a situation that demands it, an audience with the Pope, a dollar to a beggar. It is easy to find happiness, if you but look for it.

In time, your mind will learn to read that signal, that smile, as an indicator that you can live in joy. I was a deva-in-waiting for several hundred Earth years. While I awaited my final acceptance into the devic realm, I held my dream of watching communication in mind and I smiled. I celebrated life.

Life is a paradox, is it not? Only when you give up wanting, when you rest in a state of doneness, do you achieve your goal. Your smile reflects the sense of peace that fills you when you believe that whatever you would have is yours. I waited with that level of serenity and faith. If the devic kingdom had not agreed with my assessment, I would have accepted the decision and looked for another way to help other life.

What did you do while you waited?

I traveled in space and time. I studied the pyramids. I walked in silence among mummies yet undiscovered, and lived their passionate dream of Ra. I delighted in the aborigines, and blessed their dreams in this era when standardization is king. I blessed the work of novelists, poets, nonfiction writers, and essayists, as well as playwrights, speakers, and speechwriters. I made my dream real.

Tell me about your dream.

My watch is communication, and primarily I deal with words that are spoken or written for formal settings, as opposed to casual comments that you exchange with friends, family, or associates. My watch is best exemplified by poetry, the true magic in words. The term *poetry* encompasses more than words that rhyme or have meter; poetry is truth. Shakespeare's plays are poetry. Abraham Lincoln's *Gettysburg Address* is poetry, as are Franklin Roosevelt's *Fireside Chats*. Be it fiction or nonfiction, truth is your goal. I help you find your truth in the spoken or written word.

Do you stop at words? In all fields—religion, art, science, business, law, mathematics, physics, cinematography, and on and on—there are men and women who are not writing books or giving lectures, but who are searching for truth.

All they need to do is think deeply about a subject, and desire to speak their truth. Equations, paintings, photographs, and building designs are as potent as words. No earnest appeal or prayer goes unanswered in our realm. There are no barriers, no boasts of: I do this, and only this. My focus is communication, and I bless each earnest seeker of truth, in every field of endeavor.

The Guardian of Water Clarification says that words are not as accurate as shared vision, and that in time we will get rid of them.

Mine is a new post. I am convinced—and I have persuaded others—that words can heal as well as kill. They are that extreme in their power. Once you harness your communication, both spoken and written, you begin to control your thoughts and emotions.

Words reflect emotion plus thought. Say them with love, and the harshest words *are* love; say them with fear, and they can strike terror into any heart. To take an extreme example, if a rapist were to say, "I love you," you would find nothing but horror in those words; on the other hand, the same phrase spoken by a lover would ring with promise and joy. Similarly, the meaning behind the words, "We shall overcome," is vastly different when you envision them shouted by Martin Luther King and Adolf Hitler.

Words are as capable of harm as actions, and you judge them in your life review the same as you do actions.

Surely words are not as bad as actions. Out of sheer frustration, most people have said, "I could kill him," at one time or another, with no intention of harming anyone.

As far as your system of laws is concerned, what you say is true. In terms of your life evaluation after death, it may or may not be so. Your intention is the determiner. Words said in anger, with no thought of follow-through, are just words. If you have committed the crime in your mind, however, you must readdress your life script to bring your mind to a point at which it would not consider such an act. You might decide on a life as a contemplative monk. You might even plan to spend a lifetime as a person who will be murdered.

I underscore what the Guardian of Water Clarification has told you: There is no Last

Judgment by another. Saint Peter does not keep records, and neither does God; *you* keep them. Similarly, there is no heaven or hell, except as you create your own. Dante wrote lovely poetry, but the reality is that minds travel to the astral world after death, and all minds evaluate themselves there.

I speak now of humanity's questions, since they are of principal concern to you and your readers.

The first question the primary mind asks is: How close did I come to realization, both in terms of living my life purpose—the life's work most in keeping with my individual self-expression—and in terms of my awareness of God as the Creator and First Cause of my life, and all life? Religion does not matter, the groups that you joined are forgotten, your society's laws are nonessential, and even what you did in life is unimportant, except in terms of the self- and God-realization of which I speak.

The mind's second question is: How fully did I assist others, and other life? The word *others* includes your family and friends, as well as your enemies. *Other life* refers to everything you see and touch: animal, plant, and mineral. From the television in your home to the rocket booster, the humble crabgrass to the elegant orchid, the mosquito to the elephant, the evanescent puddle to the ocean, the smallest cloud to the Jet Stream, the pebble to the diamond, and the baby starving in Africa to the Vanderbilts and Rothschilds, all is of God, and, as such, all is precious.

Did you honor others, and other life, with blessings as well as with assistance? Understand that you are not obliged to save the world, but there are ways that you can reach out every day: by contributing time or money to a worthwhile cause, by calling a friend who is going through a hard time, by planting flowers or bushes that will attract and feed birds, by sending a blessing to an enemy. The options are endless.

Based on your evaluation of these essential life issues of self-, other-, and God-realization, you plan your next life. Be aware that neutralizing your judgments about others, and other life, is your first priority as you prepare this life plan. For example, if you deride the Afghans as infidels and savages, you will choose a life as an Afghan. If you, as a man, believe that women are inferior, you will choose to reincarnate as a woman.

There is no way around it: If you do not cleanse a judgment in this lifetime, you will reincarnate into the life that you focus on. Moreover, you are not limited to the human dimension. If you hate cats or evergreens, you will assign yourself lifetimes as these forms, to work out those strong negative emotions.

Ultimately, you are called to live like Jesus. Because he lived in love, not fear, he could say of those who killed him, "Father, forgive them, for they know not what they do." He accepted the appalling things that his persecutors did as being in the hands of the Creator, not him, a man among men. He did not burden himself with fear and judgment, even in the face of death. I know this is a big order, but this level of perfection is your ultimate goal.

Once you walk past fear, once you begin to live with that kind of mastery, your goal becomes one of helping other life to achieve that level of acceptance and love. Many levels of service to other life, including the devic realm, are available to you.

The Guardian of Water Clarification says that you chose to become a deva while you were still alive.

I knew of others who had made this transition, and I too made the choice to become part of this realm, with emphasis on communication. It is my best path.

Are there people making the same sorts of choices today?

Yes. We do not speak of the openings to other realms that you become aware of once you walk past fear; they are best experienced when you are ready.

Some people say you were not human, just an invention of storytellers.

I was indeed human, and I was a shaman. My father was a handsome ne'er-do-well, a soldier who left soon after I was born. My mother was a seer. She nurtured and educated me.

Concerning the woman I loved, the truth is far more prosaic than your tales of an infatuation with the Lady of the Lake. My wife, Glenwyn, died in childbirth, along with my son. I received some esoteric knowledge from my mother, but Glenwyn opened me to prophecy. She was also hauntingly lovely. Rossetti's images most closely depict her. I did not choose another.

I served as advisor for Uther Pendragon and his successor, Arthur. When it came time for my king to mount his steed in battle, I was at the forefront of the troops. I was a military man as well as a seer.

What of Excalibur, the Sword in the Stone?

I was gifted with second sight, which allowed me to see the truth behind outer appearances. That story has a grain of truth in it, but again, it is not as spectacular as the storytellers would have you believe. I saw the master key in a stone that contained a precious amethyst, and told Arthur how to best strike it to expose the flawless gemstone. Arthur then presented it to the king. I, in effect, gave the kingdom to Arthur through that vision. He was the most qualified for leadership, both in heart and mind.

Books give us a reasonably clear picture of how you lived during Arthur's time. Tell me about your life after that.

By the time Arthur was ready to leave his body, I was close to one hundred years old. I realized that there was no limit to my lifespan. I grew up with a clairvoyant mother and I married a soothsayer. I learned their lore and was given the time to perfect it.

I was one of a group of pilgrims who discovered the key to long life. We decided to retire to the Alps. I assure you that we traveled from England by conventional means, not broomsticks! I do not say where we settled, or if our community still exists. Since we were essentially self-sufficient and lived at a distance from the small villages in the region, our longevity did not attract undue attention.

I communicated through dream images with the kings that succeeded Arthur. That is how my legend as a soothsayer grew. Some were open to my advice; others were not. In time, they became less receptive and I less giving.

You said that your span of years was unlimited. That means you decided to die.

I traveled widely in spirit, and finally stepped into this dimension. To other people, yes, the body was indeed dead, once I made the decision to transfer my primary mind—or soul—to the devic realm.

I tell you this: Everyone chooses to die.

Most of us die of one sickness or other. Are you saying that we plan to be sick?

Yes. Sickness is part of your decision to die. It represents your cooperation with the dream of dying.

Children die. I cannot believe that children are ready to die.

Yes, they are ready to die. Do not mourn their short lives. They are here for a season, to do one thing. They are part of the great cycle of reincarnation, in which each takes care of the unfinished business of other lifetimes. When Glenwyn and my child died, it took three years before I finally accepted the fact that they were here to do what was necessary for themselves, not my comfort.

Do you feel like a man or a woman now?

Since I lived for so long as a man, I identify with that gender. I have a great deal of freedom now that I have left the confines of the body. Without the physical clothing of skin, it is possible to see mind as the core truth of existence.

What do we look like to you?

Although your bodies are present, we are most interested in your minds. As your mind frees itself from fear, it fills with light and becomes transparent, much like a leaded glass window with bright sun streaming through it. When your mind is filled with fear, it is dark and opaque, much like a smoke-damaged window in a burnt-out building.

In helping you to find your truth, my blessings also help you clear your mind of fear.

This idea of expressing my truth is hard to grasp. Tell me more.

Your truth is tied into the life plan—a blueprint for your life on Earth—that you develop while you are in the astral realm. For example, Martin Luther King, Abraham Lincoln, and Mahatma Gandhi had as their truth the freedom of particular groups of people, and they developed

37

their life plans accordingly. Henry David Thoreau, Rachel Carson, and John Muir revered life other than human, and they too based their life plans on that model.

On Earth, they each felt an affinity for what they had planned, and followed through with what became a life purpose. Each contacted me through a desire to speak truth, and I blessed each search. They did the work; my blessing simply helped them open doorways in their minds. I add that none of them knew I existed. You do not have to know of my presence to receive my blessings. I bless each search, with my overall goal the steady expansion of truth in the world.

As a human, you know how easy it is to become distracted. Be aware that mental detours are always based in fear, because your search for the truth—be it the heart of a character or a situation in a story or play, or a statement of fact in a nonfiction book or on a podium—often takes you past the bounds of social norms as you perceive them. I add here that the more restricted your childhood was in terms of welcoming new ideas, the more limited is your view of what those norms should be.

In all walks of life, you must be willing to do two things in order to express your truth. First, you must look at what you consider normal squarely and recognize that you can go past that perceived limitation. Do not fear; someone else in the world thinks as you do. There are no new truths. Even Einstein's theory of relativity is a statement of an existing fact.

Second, you must believe in your truth. Unlike decisions about life and death, which you can and do control, you have no power over your work once it travels into the wider vision. Your ideas will be spat upon or they will be lauded. In the end, it does not matter what others think. What is important is your act of faith in doing your work, and the kernel of truth that you disclose. When you pair your faith with the truth found in your heart, that truth has a way of inspiring the faith of others.

Do you understand? Truth persists. That is why Emerson, Homer, and Milton endure. That is why collectors rediscovered Van Gogh's paintings many years after his death. Think of his great *Starry Skies*. You know by way of the eye of the Hubbell telescope that he uttered truth beyond his conscious knowledge in that painting. You also know from his life story that you do not have to live a blameless life—in humanity's judgment—to speak truth. All you have to do is to live true to yourself. Your inner truth is your real gift from God, along with life itself.

In the end, you have two things: faith and truth. As you live both, you grow toward transparency of being. That is a big understanding!

SECTION II
FEAR FILLS OUR LIVES

Do you plan to live in fear all your life?
You are not joyful right now
because you choose not to be joyful.
We can pray for your well-being, but only you can reach out
and unclip the velvet-covered cord that keeps you
in the Fear section of the theater of life.

Guardian of Communication

Chapter Three

JUDGMENT, THE ENTRYWAY TO FEAR

I wish to speak about fear, and, I
trust, to begin the process of
loosening its persistent grip on
your heart.

Guardian of Water Clarification

The word *persistent* bothered me. I jotted on a piece of blank paper: "I am not expecting the bogeyman to knock on the door, or a nuclear holocaust—at least not today."

The answer jolted me out of the comfortable thought that I was fearful at times—wasn't everybody?—but not often enough to be concerned about it.

* * *

What if I were to tell you that you spend
seventy-five percent of your waking hours in fear?

In other words, if I am awake for sixteen hours out of twenty-four, I am fearful for twelve of those hours?

Not all days fit that specific pattern, but on average it is true. First, let us discuss change, which is the starting point for fear. Then we will deal with love and fear. At that point, I trust this statistic will make more sense.

CHANGE IS THE BASELINE FOR ALL LIFE

Change is a deceptively simple word. You live in a world of change, which we define as flow from one state to another, either in mind or action. You see change most clearly in your immediate world. Whatever you do or think affects those who are close to you: friends, relatives, and neighbors. Similarly, their actions and thoughts impact your life.

Of course, change does not stop at the boundary of your personal world. The decisions of your town, state, or federal government; a flash flood, fire, or hurricane; or terrorist actions on the other side of the globe all affect you to a greater or lesser degree. Similarly, your thoughts of fear or love affect them, and the world as a whole.

How could I affect big events, and the planet? I am just one person.

Multiply your thoughts by those of ten million people, each of whom defines herself or himself as *one person*, and you begin to envision the answer to that question. Fear and love are cumulative.

Always be aware that change marches with a swift, sure step in every life. Can you show me one thing, including you, that remains static from day to day? If you were to revisit your home in two years, would the plants, books, paintings, and furniture all be the same as they are now?

Everything—and everyone—is part of the flow that you term age. Even such seemingly immutable entities as mountains, the Earth, the Sun, and the universe experience the effects of change.

You can react to change in one of two ways: with love or fear. We consider love first.

LOVE: ACCEPTANCE AND A SENSE OF UNION

We define *love* as your sense of acceptance and union in the face of change. You experience a sense of union when you commit yourself to another person, life form, or God; or, alternatively, to a cause, ideal, or goal. People who consider their lives most successful combine both types of commitments. Do you not feel stronger when you join your heart and mind with that of another individual, or a group of like-minded people?

Definitely. Even the hardest job seems easier.

The hardest task is easier physically, but most importantly, it is less stressful mentally. It is easy to fall into the trap of distrusting yourself and your beliefs when you stand alone. Reinforcement by another, or others, strengthens your will to achieve and helps you deal with the change that accompanies all accomplishments or decisions.

The other element of love is acceptance of the individuals who are part of your world, along with the goals that you seek or the ideals that you serve, and the change that accompanies people, situations, and issues.

45

Many people or causes have aspects that I cannot accept.

You think that acceptance means you must respond passively. That is not the case. There are three steps to acceptance. First, you acknowledge that change involving a person, situation, or issue exists. Then, as dispassionately as possible, you evaluate the foreseeable effects of that change, decide what outcome you desire, and make a choice regarding your role. Finally, you allow it to play out as it will. If a situation or issue—or person—stabilizes at a point that is not acceptable, you decide again.

For instance, someone takes charge of a project that is important to you in the workplace. You acknowledge that this situation exists, evaluate where the new manager wants to take the project, and assess the type and extent of the change you and others will experience. Is the new direction acceptable? If not, you may decide to speak with all involved in order to reach a compromise. In a week or a month, if the agreement has not worked, you have three options: go along with the new direction, again attempt to steer it to a path that is acceptable to you, or leave the project.

What about individual issues, like being short of money?

You use a variation of the same process. Many people live on the edge of poverty because of bad investments, overextended credit, loss of a job, a corporation failure, or simply not enough income. The solution is to let go of all the people, issues, and situations that you could blame: the stock market, investment analyst, boss, corporation, and yourself.

Accept that this issue exists, and realize you played a role in it. Perhaps you agreed to take a position that does not pay adequately because it was the only one you could find; perhaps you agreed to a risky investment; perhaps you knew through rumor that your company was having serious financial problems but decided to stay in your job. In the end, it does not matter.

Analyze the potential change, without judging the situation, issues, or players, including yourself; state your preferences and determine your role; and then let it go. If you are spiritually minded, give the results to God as the ultimate arbiter.

You must take this critical step of acceptance in order to see clearly and then go forward. You create your world with your thoughts. If you think you are poor, powerless, sick, or a failure; or alternatively if you think you are wealthy, powerful, healthy, and successful, you are so, no matter how much or how little wealth, power, health, and success you have by the world's standards. Your "job" is to accept everything—the enjoyable as well as the uncomfortable aspects of life—as your creation. And remember that, as a human, you are here to grow to perfection, not to be perfect, so do not add self-judgment to the mix.

Acceptance is the only thing that makes sense. Is anger directed at another person, yourself, or a corporation going to make one bit of difference in the outcome as it now stands? Your solution lies in going forward.

FEAR: JUDGMENT AND A SENSE OF SEPARATION

If *acceptance* and *union* are the words that characterize love, *judgment* and *separation* epitomize fear. We define *fear* as the sense of separation that arises the moment you judge any change, big or small, past or future, as bad or good, wrong or right.

You may have a hundred other people in your life; you may be committed to goals, ideals, or God. However, once you create a state of duality by making a judgment, you stand alone. The commitment that you felt to another or to a cause is shattered.

For example, marriage partnerships often break up as the ideal expressed in the wedding vows gives way to everyday reality, revealing to both partners a person different from the one they envisioned. Will you judge the other, or accept that this person is in your life for a reason? Once you make your first judgment, it is easy to judge again, and more harshly; in time, there seems to be nothing left to save, no remnant of the sense of union and acceptance that you once felt for the other.

I think of a judgment as an opinion that I form after I think about an issue, situation, or person.

Consider judgments ultimatums, rather than opinions, with no room for dissension or movement.

Why is calling someone *good* a problem? And, for that matter, what is the problem with *right*?

> The problem is that these words set up a polarity. The reason that you retreat to polarities is that you are afraid of change. You are presented with a situation or issue that brings change into your life, and you judge it—and the person behind it—based on your reaction to the change.
>
> The moment you make a judgment, you become fearful. Moreover, you are almost never fearful for the reasons you think.

Even in the example of the marriage partnership?

> Yes. Your judgment of bad or good, wrong or right may center on your marriage partner, but he is not the real target, it is the change that he introduces.
>
> The vital thing to remember about judgments is that there are no such things as ultimatums. I offer two examples. When Galileo proposed that the Sun was the center of the Solar System, rather than the Earth, he frightened Church authorities, who could not see beyond the ripples that his theory would cause in existing religious thought. Their reaction was to judge his work as wrong and him as bad. In the early part of the past century, your government decreed that the consumption of alcohol was wrong and subsequently enacted laws making it illegal. How would you label both of these judgments?

At the time, the authorities must have thought they were correct. Now they seem hopelessly outdated.

Exactly. Even polar opposites are really just stopping points on a circle. At what point does right become wrong, or good become bad? Some people consider abortion wrong, but is it wrong when a pregnancy endangers the life of the mother, or when the fetus dies in the womb? You can try to draw arbitrary lines as an individual, a church, or a society, in order to create order from seeming chaos, but you are simply defining the part of the circle on which you will stand, and that place becomes modified as ideas shift.

I add that you are entitled, and that indeed you have the built-in drive to make these kinds of decisions. The problem arises when you believe that they are permanent and that they represent the only correct way of thinking. That rigidity is the cause of judgments, which escalate to discord and strife, from fistfights to wars.

The truth is that whenever you choose a stopping point, you also have to deal with its opposite. You only free yourself by accepting both.

Are you saying that if I decide to become a peace activist, I have to support war?

You do not have to embrace war; instead, you accept that others believe war is necessary, rather than judge them. You recognize the mindset that plans and carries out wars as part of the human condition. Then, as dispassionately as possible, you evaluate the change that you foresee if those who propose war have their way, choose the outcome you prefer, and determine your role.

In this case, you become a peace activist from acceptance, not judgment.

Finally, you allow the situation to play out as it will. If it escalates to a point that is unacceptable, you go through the steps of acceptance again. Perhaps you will decide on a new role in your community or in the nation.

Some things are givens, such as the commandment, Thou shalt not kill.

The commandment would seem to represent certainty. However, those who break certain laws—including the one against killing—are often executed, soldiers are trained to kill your nation's enemies, and your country has mounted punitive strikes against nations that threaten it.

The same is true of every statement that would seem to resolve a duality. The exceptions to the rule are honored as much as, and sometimes more than, the rule itself. For example, the commandment, Thou shalt not covet thy neighbor's wife, is generally considered an individual concern, at least until it becomes an issue in a divorce proceeding.

You are saying that, in effect, there are no rules.

There are no fixed standards, no moral imperatives; all you have are commonly agreed-upon stopping points that are subject to reinterpretation and change. Without the need for interpretation, you would have no lawyers, and you know that the law is not an endangered profession!

DESIRE LIES BEHIND ALL CHANGE

It is necessary to address desire, which is the emotion that lies behind acceptance and judgment of change. Commonly, people think of desire only in the sexual sense; we widen that definition to include a yearning for a particular outcome: personal, professional, or societal. You want another home, you look for a new car, you demand a raise in pay, you wish your husband or wife would behave differently in large or small ways, you pray for peace on Earth.

At the point at which you recognize a desire, either yours or another person's, recognize that every desire involves change. You now have two choices: You can judge the desire, and the change that it introduces, as bad or good, wrong or right, or you can accept it.

I restate the three steps to acceptance. First, you recognize that change exists, and that it is based in desire. Then, as dispassionately as possible, you evaluate the change that you foresee, visualize your ideal outcome, and make a decision regarding your role. Finally, you let the change play out as it will.

For example, you wish to buy a home. Let us use that desire as our jumping-off point.

I may wish for a home, but if I cannot afford it, why bother thinking about it?

It sounds as if you have judged yourself as wrong for wanting a new home. Is there something inherently wrong with that desire? Will home ownership damage other people or other life? As you evaluate the change that your desire will bring about, it is important to consider its effects.

There would be no particular ill effects.

What I am pointing out is that you do not have to judge desires as bad or wrong, or even good or right. All you need to do is accept the fact that you want a home. If, on reviewing your income, you decide that it is not possible to purchase it now, you have made no judgments, just taken an unbiased look at your bank balance.

With acceptance, you leave a door open to achieving your desire in a nonstandard way; with judgment, you close it. What if you were offered the chance to house-sit for a year, with a stipend for doing so? You might be able to save enough money for a down payment.

If I accept the fact that I would like to have a home despite my bank balance, then I am judging my desire as good or right.

The fact that you set up a duality that says something is good or right, as opposed to bad or wrong, is a sign of the defensive thinking that accompanies judgment. Here are some statements: *Other people have homes, and I deserve one too;* or *my home is too small, and I need a new one, despite the cost.* Do you sense the fear under those statements?

On the other hand, you can acknowledge that the desire exists and make plans to deal with the accompanying change: in this case, the need for a down payment. You still believe that you need a larger home, but you do not judge—and fear—the change that your desire will introduce into your life. Acceptance opens you to possibilities. You may decide to save a certain amount each month, look for house-sitting situations, or the like.

A judgment would not preclude making those kinds of decisions.

Assume that any judgment can mire you in fear, because it sets up polarities. Judgments *always* lead to fear.

FEAR OF CHANGE UNDERLIES ALL JUDGMENTS

Your statement about judgments brings us back to the concept of change. Any modification, adjustment, or alteration in your life or the lives of those you love, or in an ideal or goal, has within it an element of the unknown, and of risk.

Let us consider two extremes: being condemned to die within the hour in the electric chair and buying that new home. The first represents change that most people would judge as bad and the second as good, yet both can equally saturate you with fear. Once you judge these changes, you experience a heightening of all five senses, as well as an intensified chemical flow in your bloodstream—the fight-or-flight response. These fear-chemicals are corrosive to all parts of your body and mind in the same way that rust wears away the metal parts of an automobile.

I can understand how the electric chair would terrify me, but a new home would be a source of joy.

> In other words, you would judge the second situation as good. I ask you this: What would concern you, if you were buying a home?

Hidden defects showing up after I buy it.

> So, you judge the idea of buying a home as good, and the hidden problems that it might have as bad. In this case, you need to accept all the changes that accompany this type of investment—more room, its potential for appreciation, and the extra costs that you may have to shoulder—and then make your decision.

There have to be levels of fear, from anxiety to panic. Buying a home might cause some anxiety, but facing the electric chair would be a source of pure panic.

> There are no levels of fear. Whether you feel uneasy or terrified, you experience identical emotional and physical reactions. In fact, if you were a condemned person who has accepted the change termed death, you might feel more peaceful than you would about the new home.

Time has to play a big role. Moving in a month has to feel different than knowing I will be dead in an hour.

Fear does not heighten with proximity. Anxiety about change in the future, such as that new home, is as real, as imminent, as the fear you would feel walking to the electric chair. When you become fearful, you become fully charged with fear, and it does not diminish with time.

What about change we cannot help but judge as bad, such as the catastrophic hurricane in New Orleans or the devastation of the World Trade Center?

The effects of natural or manmade disasters are horrendous for those caught in them. You can judge the situation as bad and enter the realm of fear, or you can accept the destruction without judging it; it is your choice. What is most important—to you as well as to those affected by the tragedy—is the role that you decide to play.

Judgment, and the fear that accompanies it, can be paralyzing. For example, if you judge the people of New Orleans as bad for not leaving their city before the hurricane struck, are you likely to offer assistance to those in need? Once you accept rather than judge, once you realize that you too could be caught in an untenable choice, you are more likely to get on to the practical matter of deciding how you can help.

Is there a difference between judging a person and judging his behavior? A good person can behave badly in some situations.

Judgment of a person and judgment of her behavior are identical. Inevitably a judgment leads back to a person. Even if you are judging community or societal ills, are you not ultimately judging the mayor or the president?

Consider the situation of a mother who discovers that her son has been stealing. She has two options. She can judge the situation, and ultimately the child, as bad, and enter the realm of fear. She might feel powerless to deal with his behavior; in that sense, she would be afraid of him. Additionally, she might fear retribution by his victims. Her reaction undoubtedly would be anger: at him for putting the family in this type of situation, and at herself for not foreseeing it.

Alternatively, she can accept the fact that her son's actions have affected others and that restitution is necessary. She would then sit down with him to create a plan for repayment. In this second situation, she has not judged him as bad or his actions as wrong.

Now do you understand the statistics that I quoted earlier? Granted, you are not facing annihilation today, but you have many opportunities to be fearful.

THE JUDGMENT CIRCLE

Sometimes I am at the receiving end of another person's judgment. Certainly that is not my issue.

It may or may not be so. When Christ told his followers to turn the other cheek, what he was really saying was to walk away from judgment. If you can do that, the other person's judgment is not your issue. However, if someone judges you or your ideas and you judge that person in turn, you have entered the realm of fear. As the recipient of the initial judgment, you can be considered passive; but when you judge the other person, you become aggressive. So, you play both roles.

Whatever role you play initially, consider yourself a fear-magnet when you make a judgment. In other words, you choose fear to complete your life.

I am going to use a suitcase filled with fifty pounds of rocks as a metaphor for this fear-baggage—and note that we are not discussing a suitcase full of diamonds, just garden-variety granite. Both the instigator and recipient of fear carry such baggage. The outer form may vary, but the contents are the same.

Not only do you accomplish nothing by hauling this heavy load from place to place, you also become weary and sore, and you progress much more slowly than you would without it. Moreover, you must walk carefully, so you do not stumble; you stare at your shoes instead of the wide expanse of sky. Most important, once you carry your own fear-suitcase, you are much more likely to accept fear burdens from others.

Fear clouds your perception of alternatives, as well as your belief in your capabilities. The only way to see the wider world is to put down your fear-baggage every day. If you remember just one thing, make it this: You have to choose fear, and you choose fear the moment you make a judgment.

THE POWER OF CHOICE

Choices can be considered judgments too.

No. We define *choice* as your selection among alternatives, recognizing them as preferences, not laws.

Albert Schweitzer is one of my heroes. In *Reverence for Life*, he talks about destroying a virus to save a human life. Wasn't his choice based on the judgment that people are more important than viruses?

He made that choice through acceptance, not judgment. He chose his stopping point on the circle of life—he would save people—but he also honored the viruses that he killed.

Understand that there is no such thing as a harmless life. Every day you eat plants and animals, and your house destroys habitat for native species; the same was true for Schweitzer. Instead, he lived a blameless life. He weighed the consequences of his actions, and he chose the path that contained the least damage to other life, as well as honor for the life that he destroyed.

Before you judge or accept, you choose to do so. To use an extreme example, you could make the following decision: *Although I have been told I will die within six months, I choose to live.* You do not judge the diagnosis as bad or good, wrong or right.

Having made your choice, you do two things: you accept the event—death—as a possibility, a potential outcome based on your reality this moment; and you acknowledge that the present reality can be changed if you do not, in effect, close the door to change with judgment. If you really mean what you say, if you truly do not close the door on your choice through judgment, you can have what you choose. Your mind and will are *that* powerful. You hear about cases of spontaneous remission of serious illness. Remission only occurs when you choose it.

Remember, you *always* choose. It is part of the human condition, and beyond, it is a truth of all life. However, you *never* need to judge; you can choose acceptance instead, and walk into change without fear.

When I say "without fear," I do not mean that you feel nothing. The reality of Christ's years as a master-teacher in the Middle East was that he lost scores of followers who were dear to him. Many deserted him during his demonstrations of miracles; his ability to contact God directly frightened them.

Jesus felt this abandonment intensely, along with the urge to judge those who left him. He chose to accept his desire to judge, and then gave it to God, rather than entering fear by labeling himself or others as bad or good, wrong or right. His self-acceptance was the key to his acceptance and forgiveness of others.

The only way you can clear yourself from all issues brought up by change is to acknowledge the emotions—the desires—that you have, state your preferences, determine your role, and then, like Jesus, release all. At that point, you have achieved acceptance.

Realistically, how can anyone accept Hitler?

Let us look at the process of choice and acceptance again, with Adolf Hitler as our example. First comes the person, situation, or issue that introduces change into your life: You read about his deeds in a history book. You are surprised. Yes, even something as seemingly undemanding as reading a book can introduce change, which we define as a transformation—or potential transformation—in your way of thinking or your way of life.

Now you enter the realm of choice. If you choose to judge him as bad, you become fearful. If you choose to accept him, you acknowledge the fact that his mindset, which sees those who are different as bad, has existed throughout the timeline of history. At that point, you state your desire to unite all people and then choose to do your part to eliminate the attitude that produced this type of leadership by becoming a peace activist. Acceptance does not preclude action. You decide to play a role in changing the human condition.

It seems to me that if I were to judge Hitler as bad, my decision to become a peace activist would be stronger than if I accept that his mindset has existed throughout the timeline of history. Acceptance sounds too cerebral.

If you look closely at your life, you will find that all human tendencies are within you. You have commented that many people say, "I could kill him," at one time or another.

61

Yes, but most people do not mean it.

> Even though they do not act on it, they have the tendency; otherwise, they would never say—or, more importantly, consider—the option of killing another person. It would not be part of their thinking. With that understanding, is it not easier to accept the desire to kill on the part of another, even one who killed multitudes of innocent people?

All right, what if I encounter a mugger with a switchblade? How could I possibly accept him?

> That is a fine example. According to Tai Chi and other martial arts, what is your best reaction when faced with danger?

You are right: I need to center. If I become fearful, I have lost any chance to deal with my attacker.

> Absolutely. If you want to get away, or if you decide to fight the mugger, you must have the clear mind that centering—a facet of acceptance—provides.

Here are some questions that do not have clear-cut answers. Is it wrong or right to increase trade with China, in light of their civil rights record? Will a proposed interstate highway be bad or good for our town? How does acceptance work in these cases?

> One of the great gifts of acceptance is your ability to step back and see the big picture. China wishes to increase trade without changing its stance on civil rights, so your question is whether

that country's ethical underpinnings, as your nation sees them, should influence that decision. Do you see how looking at the big picture takes the question away from thoughts that could lead to blame of individuals, such as China's leaders?

You accept the issue as it stands, state your wish for equality of all, and then make a decision regarding how you will act in regard to it. Perhaps you will write a letter to your local newspaper; perhaps you will give to one of the many humanitarian organizations trying to influence change on the global level. The same type of thought process can be applied to the nearby highway.

The point is to step back far enough to impersonalize the data about an issue or situation so you can accept it—and the person behind it—without blame, and then make a choice based on the facts as you know them.

Letting people, situations, and issues go without judgments seems impossible sometimes.

On the other hand, what do you gain by keeping them close to you with judgments? Your goal is to see them clearly, decide what outcome you would prefer and the role you will play, and then let them go.

When I choose and accept, rather than choose and judge, will I be happy?

Happiness is one of the attributes of love, so you are really asking if you will live in love.

The answer is that you have taken the first step toward living in love.

This step is powerful beyond your ability to recognize right now. When you, along with one-tenth of the people now alive on the planet, decide to choose acceptance rather than judgment, you will change not only your destiny as a species but also the future of all life. You will end societal and environmental destruction, from wars to the rape of the rainforests.

WHAT TYPES OF JUDGMENTS DO YOU HABITUALLY MAKE?

Now look at the types of judgments that you routinely make. Judgments can be as fine as gossamer but as confining as the strongest chain when they become a habitual part of your thinking.

Once you choose to judge, rather than accept, for a hundred times, judgment becomes a habit. You may try other ways of looking at situations, issues, and people, but you deflect them, because they force you to make conscious, rather than subconscious, choices.

Your object is to recognize how many familial and societal maxims and prejudices you harbor without thinking about them.

Judgments in Your Personal Life

For one week, examine your thoughts regarding five or more situations and issues—and the people behind them—that crop up in your personal world: family, friends, neighbors, community, and workplace. At home, you may get annoyed at your child or partner regularly for some reason. At work, you may hate a coworker, or you may be fearful every time you have to give a speech or prepare a report. Behind these thoughts lie habitual judgments, such as, *I am not smart enough to talk in front of others;* or *he is a fool.*

First, state the change that the issue or situation brings up, and name the person behind it. Then state your desired outcome. Will you judge or accept it—and the person whom you deem guilty?

What about neutral situations or issues? I am going to buy groceries because I have company coming. It is not a source of judgment or acceptance.

There are no neutral situations or issues. Will you allow me to scan your thoughts?

Yes.

You plan to prepare a holiday dinner for friends. Because you received an unexpected bill of close to three hundred dollars yesterday, you fear that you will not have enough money to cover both expenses this month. You blame yourself for getting into this situation.

You are right. I reproach myself for not setting aside money for car repairs that I knew I would need. Still, I am happy that my friends are coming, even though it means added expense.

Which feeling is strongest?

My happiness at seeing old friends.

Then note both your acceptance and your judgment, with the understanding that acceptance is strongest. Also note the issue behind today's fear: your dwindling savings. You must face that concern. Remember that your mind played a role in creating the situation that you are in, so it is strong enough to create an alternate vision of you as prosperous.

Judgments in Regard to Your Nation and the World

Similarly, examine five situations and issues that you encounter in news broadcasts and newspaper articles. When you hear the name of a place such as Iraq or Harlem, what stereotypes does it bring up? If you are a Republican and you find out that someone is a Democrat or a Libertarian, what is your reaction?

How Much Time Do You Spend In Judgment?

At the end of the week, estimate how much time you spent in judgment and acceptance. The results may surprise you.

Recognize that you receive a gift in this process of uncovering judgments. Once you bring them to conscious awareness, you begin to make new choices.

Chapter Four

WHY WE CHOOSE TO LIVE IN FEAR

I come in peace to remind
you that you will die, and, in doing
so, to remind you how to live.

Guardian of Water Clarification

As I looked over my notes about those suitcases filled with granite, I realized I had not asked two key questions of the Guardian of Water Clarification: When did I first choose to carry this burden of fear? And why do I continue to carry it, if it damages body and mind?

* * *

What initially prompted me to live in fear?

You chose to carry your burden of fear as a child, and you continue to carry it as an adult, because you want to be loved. Of course, you cannot find this great gift of spirit when you are buried in fear. However, you continue to seek it there, because you were taught by your family and your society that the sense of separation that characterizes fear is the way to gain love.

Why do we think that way?

67

If someone whom you trust tells you that black is white a hundred times, you begin to accept that possibility. When others echo her opinion, you become more convinced. Of course, black is not white, no matter how many people swear on oath that it is so.

The same concept holds true for living in fear. It is not true that you can attain love by living in fear, but when people whom you have faith in—your parents or guardians, teachers, friends, and relatives—live that belief, you begin to accept it as gospel. Most people live this way.

Understand that no one deliberately plans to lie to you; they really believe that fear is the pathway to love. Judgment gives them a sense of safety, which they deem to be a state of love. You have heard people call others fools because they consider them too accepting of situations, issues, and people. It is an endless circle.

THE UNATTAINABLE GIFT OF FEAR: LOVE

How do I get out of this circle of fear?

Recognizing what you are doing is the first, and most important, step past fear. To take that step, you need to examine your search for love as a child and as an adult. That search defines you as a person.

First, what image does the term *childhood* evoke for you? What ideal of childhood exists in your mind?

I picture the ideal childhood as a time of exploration, when everything is waiting to be discovered, with caring people to comfort and guide you.

> Childhood, as you describe it, implies the presence of a strong outside authority whose gifts are stability, safety, and a sense of being loved, along with the freedom to explore new avenues, to experience joy and a sense of magic. Such a child anticipates the adventure of each new day.

On the other hand, I do not know anyone who had that kind of childhood. Where do we get these ideas?

> They are hardwired in. Babies come into the world from the astral dimension, in which they experience the loving presence of God. They choose to incarnate for specific reasons, but they also expect the love that accompanied them in the astral plane to be part of their Earth experience.
>
> Human parents often disappoint their children in this regard. Most parents carry mental baggage from their past, in the form of assaults on their spirits—their own suitcases filled with granite, if you will. So, most children grow up in an environment that is permeated with judgment, and they in turn learn to judge others—and to live in fear.
>
> The primary fear that children face is powerlessness, and their key fear behavior is anger. We will discuss these fears and behaviors in detail later.

I understand powerlessness—children have little say in their lives—but are they *that* angry?

Yes. Children cry out against the dishonor of their bodies, minds, and spirits; and against the abuse of other life that they recognize as such, particularly animals. Let us examine two examples from your life. When you were a toddler, your mother died. When you were seven, you walked half a mile to the police station to report a car that crushed a squirrel. You hated your mother for dying, and you despised the person who took that small life, then drove away.

As a child, you feel everyday horrors much more strongly than you do as an adult. You gradually learn to close your mind to them by rationalization, a form of mental gymnastics. You reason thusly as an adult: *It was my mother's time to die, and the person who ran over the squirrel probably did not see it dart into the roadway.* That is why you do not remember childhood anger.

Both of those explanations probably are true.

We are not discussing truth or falsehood here; we are talking about anger that arises at a time in your life when you have no mental armor in place to deflect it. Unless you confront childhood feelings of powerlessness and anger, you internalize them.

Physically, they are often the cause of sickness in later life. Mentally, you live in the fears and fear behaviors of childhood, no matter how old you are or how well you hide them from yourself. In turn, you inflict them on others,

70

particularly children, who are open, vulnerable, unable to defend themselves.

If I could forgive my mother for dying and the driver for running over the squirrel, could I free myself from the sense of powerlessness and rage that I felt as a child?

Those parts of it, yes. We will discuss the life portrait that you create as a child and refine as an adult. Once you understand and come to peace with that portrait, you begin to cleanse your fear.

First, though, we must talk about your search for love as an adult. You can think of it as a continuation of your childhood quest for love; in fact, your life portrait as an adult contains many of the same behaviors that you developed as a child. Remember that even the most extreme fear behavior is really a call for one or more of the gifts of a life lived in love: certainty, strength, unity, happiness, peace, stability.

Was Adolf Hitler searching for love?

His primary goals were stability, unity, and power for his country. He sought to achieve those goals by eliminating people and ideas that did not meet his standards and by conquering other nations. You see how warped the search for the gifts of love can become when they are powered by fear.

YOUR LIFE PORTRAIT DICTATES HOW YOU LIVE

Did you have a comfortable life after your mother died?

71

When my father remarried, I had a hard time fitting into his new family.

> And you think you did not feel rage concerning your mother's death? As an adult, you may have come to peace with the fact, but not the emotion behind it. Your first step to liberation is to acknowledge—and accept—that you judged her as bad for dying. You also carried guilt about her death; we will examine that later.
>
> Along similar lines, do you not feel pain about the plight of animals to the point that you support several wildlife organizations?

Yes, I do.

> A competent counselor could work with you to trace that concern back to the incident with the squirrel. My point is this: If you never come to peace with the pain of your childhood, it affects you until you die. Childhood is when you create your life portrait, which you carry with you into old age.

What does the term *life portrait* mean?

> Think of it as you would a portrait on canvas. It is what you believe is the essential *you*, and you use it as your baseline for interactions with others. You, and others around you, see this portrait as you, but, similarly to a work on canvas, it can be changed.
>
> In childhood, you gain a perception of yourself as loved or unloved, as obedient or

disobedient, as active or passive, as a successful or unsuccessful student, and as a bully, victim, or a person who stands up for her rights. This portrait forms the basis of how you think of yourself as an adult, and your thoughts translate into your life experiences. Even your overall pattern of sickness and health is often based on adult illnesses that you experienced second-hand as a child.

Are you saying that a person might develop heart disease because she believes she will get it, not because of genetic patterning?

Genetic patterning may be a factor, but it is less important than mind patterning. Did not a friend tell you that he wanted to die at fifty?

Yes, and he died of a stroke at fifty-two.

Did not a family friend who feared that she had cancer die of the disease twenty years after she first started seeing oncologists? The fact that she showed no signs of cancer until several years before her death means that she chose the disease for seventeen years before she developed it.

But isn't it possible that both of these people knew the truth about themselves? They may not necessarily have chosen to die.

What is the difference? You can always make another choice. I use the physicist Stephen Hawking as an example. Does he not choose to live in spite of the doctors' predictions? Choice is the ultimate arbiter of your life, and the experiences that you have in childhood, adulthood, and, to a lesser extent, previous lives, influence those choices.

The portrait of yourself that you create as a child, and reinforce as an adult, is your guide. For example, if you created a life portrait of yourself as a so-so student and someone dismisses a report that you prepare, you may be tempted to throw it out. If, on the other hand, you created a life portrait of yourself as a good student and a person who fights for her rights, you may defend your work.

THE REAL GIFTS OF FEAR

If fear is a dead-end, there have to be reasons why generation after generation of people continue to choose it.

As we have discussed, most people are not aware that love is unattainable if they continue to live in fear. Even those who do recognize that truth may stay immersed in fear, because it offers three major gifts.

The first gift has to do with life and death. Most people believe that they will die if they are not fearful. Think of it this way: If you are a fish, it is natural to live in water; your life and your vision are entwined with water. If a turtle tells you that she lives in air as well as water, would you believe her? Given that most of humanity lives in fear more or less continually, it seems as essential to you as water does to the fish. What happens when you let fear go? Will you die?

The second gift—a sense of safety—is related to the first. Given that most of humanity lives in fear, you have the sense of walking in step with your brothers and sisters. This is a huge reward; do not discount it. At the same time, you have a feeling of safety for the opposite reason: When you are fearful, you feel separate from everyone and everything else. There is a consolation in that feeling. Even if others intrude on your life, they cannot control your thoughts. The concept of All Is One is frightening.

The third and greatest gift is the illusion of controlling change. Once you judge an event, situation, or issue, you do not have to think about it—or the person behind it—any longer. Let us address the World Trade Center nightmare. If you judge the CIA as wrong for not having averted the tragedy, do you want to help the victims, or do you feel justified in putting all the responsibility on the government?

WHAT LIFE PORTRAIT DID YOU DEVELOP AS A CHILD?

I ask you now to examine your life as a child, before you reached puberty. What you carry with you from this time of your life, when you look to others to teach you what it means to be an adult, is key to your behavior patterns in later life.

Family Dynamics

Take a close look at your family dynamics. Did you feel loved or unloved? Did your parents or guardians respect your talents and abilities, or did they dismiss your achievements? Did they set aside enough time to be with you, or did you feel neglected? Did they face the world confidently, or did they seem to be fearful?

Personality

Think about your childhood personality patterns. Were you considered obedient or disobedient, or a mix of the two? Did you make friends easily, or were you a loner? Were you a leader or a follower? Did you feel successful or unsuccessful as a student? Were you sick much of the time? Were you a bully, a victim, or somewhere in the middle?

Other Issues

Note other positives and negatives. What types of things did you excel at, or did you enjoy, even if you did not stand out? Did you have abilities in a particular area, such as sports, music, science, or art? What types of things did you dislike, or do badly? Are there childhood situations, issues, or people that still trouble you, or that you look back on fondly?

WHAT LIFE PORTRAIT HAVE YOU CREATED AS AN ADULT?

This portrait of your childhood is a pointer to your life as an adult: your strengths, as well as your core fears and fear behaviors. For example, if you were not an honored member of your family, a core fear could be powerlessness. As a result, you may try to control every aspect of your world, or you may obsessively seek others to complete your life, rather than relying on yourself.

If your family did not believe in, and promote, your talents and abilities, a core fear could be failure. As a result, you may lash out in anger toward others, or be depressed, which indicates anger at self.

If you grew up in a family that never believed that they had enough, a core fear could be lack. As a result, you may choose frenzied activity as a way to avoid it, or alternatively live in the imagined glories or sorrows of the past or the future, rather than face the present. We will consider each of the primary fears and fear behaviors in detail.

Before we examine them, however, I ask you to look for areas in which your actions and thoughts are outgrowths of those that you had as a child, as well as areas in which you have made changes.

Level of Happiness

How does your level of happiness compare with what you experienced as a child? What types of situations, issues, and people bring up feelings of happiness or unhappiness? Do they correlate with your experiences in childhood?

Work

Are you doing work that you love, or working for other reasons? Did family members do work that they loved? Do you feel the same about work that you did about school? Do you echo your family's attitude toward work?

Money

What is your connection with money? Are you rich, poor, or in-between? How would you live ideally? How does your present life relate to your family's attitude toward prosperity?

Health Issues

Are you usually sick or healthy? Do you believe that you have a predilection for a certain illness or injury, because it runs in the family? Are there illnesses or injuries that you do *not* feel you will "inherit"? Are there any benefits to being sick?

Relationships

Overall, do you feel successful or unsuccessful in your relationships with family and friends? Which relationships feel successful and which feel unsuccessful? Are there ways to resolve the unsuccessful ones? Do the number and quality of your relationships mirror what you or your family experienced when you were a child?

In general, what has changed and what has stayed the same? Are there ways that you can address areas in which you feel stagnant or unfulfilled?

It is one thing to read about fear in a book and have a feeling that some of the concepts may apply to you. What I am asking you to do is to make those ideas personal. It is a vital part of your journey through fear.

Chapter Five

STOPPING FEAR AT JUDGMENT

> One negative judgment ripples
> into all areas of your life. You
> need to allow love to permeate
> every corner of your mind and
> your heart.

> Guardian of Communication

My most pressing concern was: How do I stop fear in its tracks, once I make a judgment? The Guardian of Communication answered my unspoken question.

* * *

It is not possible to stop fear at the point of judgment until you are willing, as Christ said, to "go and sin no more." You can think of *sin* as any judgment you make of another person—and, as we have discussed, judgments are ultimately of people.

Judgment is a tricky companion, in that you often feel forced to judge in order to keep your sense of self intact. It is important to understand that you are not dealing with your true self.

There is a part of you that always lives in acceptance and union; think of it as a built-in program. Union, or love, is what lies at the end of your journey through fear. It is not something that you add on; it is something you uncover. Whether you call this state of union happiness, joy, or peace, you are dealing with an aspect of the umbrella term, *love*. It is your birthright, part of what you carry with you from the astral world, along with the blueprint that you created for your life.

I find this hard to believe. There is so much evil in the world.

What you perceive as evil is the result of fear. It does not live in its own right. From stress at a planetary level to fear at an individual level, all of what you perceive as evil around you is a demonstration of fear in action.

The opposite of fear is love. It is that simple. You carry a built-in program to live in love, and you overlay it with fear. Master-teachers, such as Jesus, did not live in fear; they reached a state in which love predominates. What one person can do, all people can do.

You create fear in order to cope with the dualities involved in living. Few people have static lives; they experience sickness and health, success and failure, lack and abundance, powerlessness and strength at various stages of their lives. And everyone experiences the most polarizing of all dualities, birth and death. Fear is your creation to deal with these dualities.

On the other hand, if God created everything, then dualities are included. That means they must have a purpose, but what is it?

> Without dualities, you would lose the great gift of freedom of choice. You are like the beggar in the old tale, who asked for a meal and received a fishing pole instead. By handing you a fishing pole—in this case, your choice to bypass the effects of dualities by walking past fear—God allows you to live as a free person. I live as I do by choice, not programming.

What about calamities such as earthquakes, volcanoes, and the like? Where do they fit into this picture?

> Your power of mind is vast enough to counter stresses in the Earth. Humanity could literally reroute a massive flow of magma or divert a hurricane out to sea with the power of mind.

Are you implying that the people of Pompeii brought on the eruption of Mount Vesuvius?

> It is not that simple or direct, but yes, humanity's fear creates stresses in the planet. The Earth neutralizes natural and human-induced pressures through volcanic eruptions, storm activity, and the like.
> I do not say that if you live free of judgment, volcanoes will remain dormant; hurricanes, tornadoes, and earthquakes will be eliminated; great landmasses will no longer drift apart; or the magnetic core will remain stable. The planet needs to cleanse natural stresses that arise

from its long journey through space, in addition to those engendered by your fear. However, these disasters would be far less destructive with the power of mind directed to them, and they would be far less frequent if you lived in a state of love, rather than fear. Fully half of the Earth's stresses are powered by your fear.

Bottom-line, you can elect to create your own worldview based on fear, or you can embrace the built-in program labeled Love. Everyone eventually chooses love, if not in one lifetime, then in myriad lifetimes. It is the brass ring that you seek.

There are countless human-like planes other than this one, and on many of them, beings much like you live other aspects of the journey into love. They have replaced the physical violence and destruction caused by fear with mental control. They have developed their minds to the point at which they use them for travel to far reaches of the galaxy and universe, as well as for expanded lifespans, physical health and vitality, and the like. They are dealing with the finer points of living.

They have chosen lives on these planes to eradicate their last vestiges of fear and to live out blueprints that they have designed for their life work as scientists, explorers, and the like. On a plane such as yours, where fear is dominant, the plan often becomes subservient to the search for wealth, fame, or power.

I assume we have been visited by these beings.

Yes. All who visit the Earth possess the technology and breadth of vision that allows them to journey by means of astral laws. This means that they travel far beyond the speed of light, and they compress time.

Many do not yet have full strength of mind and will, so they must cross into the physical realm when they reach the Earth's atmosphere. Others have evolved to the point at which they, like your great earthly masters, live completely in love; they travel to Earth on the astral level. UFO sightings are of beings and ships that have entered the physical sphere from the astral; you are unaware of those that travel completely by astral means.

How many UFOs come each year?

Not as many arrive as did before you armed yourselves. In a sense, you are off-limits; they think of Earth as you do the slums of your great cities. They see you as barbarians with missiles, with all countries equally culpable.

To be specific, approximately fifteen hundred extraterrestrial vehicles enter Earth's atmosphere every year. This number represents one-tenth of those who came before the mid-twentieth century. In that sense, you have been successful in deterring them, as the scientist Von Braun predicted.

Do they want to conquer us?

They do not seek to triumph over you, but to restrain you. Their primary purpose is to keep

83

your technology, which has advanced beyond your minds, in check. Trust me, once you become aware on this level, you give up any thought about mechanical methods of destruction. You recognize that mind is much more powerful than any bomb.

What level do we, as humans, have to reach in order to choose these other planes after death?

In effect, once you free yourselves from judgments, you can live at a level that allows you to make such choices. You know of people who have achieved this level of freedom. Mahatma Gandhi, Albert Einstein, and Albert Schweitzer are examples of people who have bypassed the iron grip of fear to this degree. You do not have to be a priest or shaman to live an advanced mental life.

Beyond that, once you learn to fully live in the state of love, the cycle of rebirths, on all planes, is over. On this plane, master-teachers such as Francis of Assisi are examples of lives lived wholly in love. There are many more like Francis, living in anonymity, who literally keep the planet from imploding. Without their expressions of love, combined with ours, humanity would have eradicated all life on Earth by now.

Additionally, many who could make the transition to a realm such as ours elect to come back to your plane to help their brothers and sisters evolve to a full state of love. Jesus, Buddha, and Krishna are examples of masters who made that choice. There are many options open to you once you reach the level at which you live in love, but the overall goal is the same: to help all life evolve to a state of love. These master-teachers elected to fulfill that goal by reincarnating on Earth.

STOPPING JUDGMENT BEFORE IT BEGINS

We seemingly stray far from the topic of stopping judgment, but it is essential for you to understand the power of love, as well as the fact that love is built-in, a blueprint from God, if you will. You asked if you can call a halt to fear at the point of judgment. The answer is yes. You can even stop the judgment process before it takes root in your conscious mind. That is what master-teachers do, and it is your ultimate goal.

Recognize the Physical and Mental Signs of Judgment

Judgment signals its presence by a tightening in your abdominal, midriff, or chest area when you experience a situation or issue, as well as a person—judgment always comes back to a person—whom you would judge. This physical reaction, which varies in each person, precedes conscious awareness that you have made a judgment. With concentration, you can learn to identify it as soon as it occurs. If you can stop the judgment process before it reaches the level of thought, you have reached a high state of mental control.

Picture a person whom you do not like, or who scares you. In truth, both have the same roots; you would not be judgmental if you were

85

not fearful. Do you feel a tightening in your abdomen, midriff, or chest?

Yes. It is centered near my solar plexus.

That is a common place to feel judgment. Others include tension in the abdominal cavity, a burning sensation in or near the stomach, or a feeling of constriction in the heart area.

See Yourself in the Other

This brings us to the second step for dismantling judgment before it reaches your mind. Once you feel this burning or constriction, bring to mind the picture of the person whom you would judge.

Now, accept two things: The person is one of your kind, and you would not be making a judgment if you were not attuned to this person. By *attuned*, I refer to the fact that all emotions reside in all people. You literally are Attila the Hun and Theresa of Avila. Although you may not be a warrior bent on murdering all in your path, you have the same tendencies toward judgment, and your own ways of expressing fear through anger, control, and the like. On the other side of the coin, although you may not be a fully realized master such as Theresa, you have that predisposition as well.

If I were hiking and came face-to-face with a bear, I would feel the same reaction, but there would be no person to blame.

86

There is always a person to blame. Granted, you will not have time to do anything immediately except run, but once you are safe, you probably will feel one of the symptoms we discussed. At that point, visualize the person whom you blame—generally the first image that comes to mind when you recognize this bodily discomfort; in this case, perhaps the hike leader—see him as a fellow human being, and accept the fact that you have the same types of frailties.

Acceptance is always humbling, and always necessary.

HALTING THE JUDGMENT PROCESS

We have discussed a way of dealing with judgment before your conscious mind has labeled a person as bad or good, wrong or right. The more common situation is to become aware of a judgment that you have made.

Recognize the Physical and Mental Signs of Judgment

Again, look to your body. Do you feel a tight or burning sensation in your abdomen, midriff, or heart? That sense of constriction is your cue.

At this point, in addition to the mental picture of the person whom you dislike or fear, recognize that you have added a description of an issue or situation to go with the picture. Examples are: *The company is going to lay me off, and my supervisor did not say a word to help me keep my job;* or *if the doctor had diagnosed my illness*

87

correctly, I would not be sick today. You have
made a judgment of another person as bad or
good, wrong or right, in the context of an issue or
situation.

Accept Your Judgment

Now, accept two facts: You have made a
judgment regarding a change or an impending
change, and you believe your judgment is
justified. Note the sense of satisfaction that
accompanies every judgment. Even though your
doctor misdiagnosed your illness, do you not feel
a sense of moral superiority by labeling him
wrong? On the other side of the coin, if a friend
serves your dreams at the price of setting aside
hers, do you not feel a similar sense of dominance
as you label her good?

See Yourself in the Other

Now, begin to dismantle the judgment.
First, acknowledge that you have an affinity to
what, and whom, you judge. If you blame another
for stealing, is it because you or a family member
have been similarly tempted in the past? The
person whom you judge is calling up some
echoes.

State the Results That You Would Have, and Let Go of the Situation or Issue

Finally, unveil the desire that lies under
your judgment by stating what you would have,
and then let it go. You may have to revisit your

decision in time, but there is nothing you can do about it now.

Calling a halt to judgment, whether it is in the first, or feeling, stage, or in the second stage, in which you have already judged another, can save you much grief. You do not experience the core fear-pairs, which we will discuss next, nor do you act out fear behaviors.

By this action alone, you begin to join those who are helping to heal the world.

When I am able to do this, how much fear will I cut off that original seventy-five percent of each day that I spend in fear?

If you can stop fear at the point of judgment, you eliminate close to ninety percent of all fear.

What about the remaining ten percent?

We have not discussed emotional residues, which you pick up from other people. We will talk about them when we consider ways to eradicate the fear-pairs (chapter 10).

SECTION III
THE CORE AND PRIMAL FEAR-PAIRS

Of all the forces on Earth, fear is the most deadly.
It is worse than a catastrophic earthquake in its destruction,
far wider than the largest hurricane in its path.

Guardian of Communication

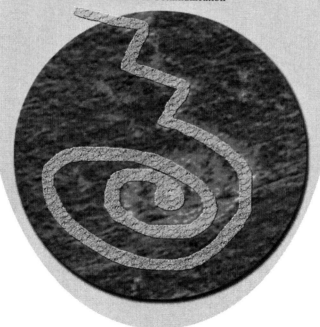

Chapter Six

THE CORE FEAR-PAIR OF POWERLESSNESS AND STRENGTH

You can be in one place or many,
and still you never outrun fear.
Fear is the enemy.

Guardian of Communication

Given what the guardian said—I had never neutralized childhood anger at my mother for dying—I went through the steps for eradicating judgments described in the previous chapter. I unearthed a burden of guilt: a two-year-old's belief that I had somehow "killed" her. I was not told that she died of complications related to pneumonia until years later. How much fear had I buried behind that judgment, and how had it affected my life with my new family?

* * *

I assume that I become fearful immediately after I make a judgment.

> Yes. If you do not stop the judgment process, you become fearful. The process is automatic and unavoidable. As a child, you judged yourself as bad, and you have carried the fear associated with that judgment since then.

The first fear-pair that anyone—adult or child—experiences is that of powerlessness and strength. I call it a fear-pair, because both sides are always present. There are four other major fear pairs that you can face after making a judgment—sickness and health, aging and youth, lack and abundance, and failure and success—but they are all variations on the theme of powerlessness and strength.

Additionally, the primal fear-pair of life and death comes into play once you make a judgment. I call it a primal fear-pair, because it lurks behind all other fears. Any fear-pair carries with it a strong fear of life and death.

We will consider each fear-pair in turn, starting with powerlessness and strength. In other words, if you feel powerless, you feel strong, and vice versa.

Describe how I can experience both at the same time.

First, let us define the terms. In this context, *powerlessness* is your sense of ineffectiveness, incompetence, and futility when you are confronted with change. A situation, issue, or person introduces change, or the potential for change, and you are ready to give up before you face it—or him, or her. *Strength*, on the other hand, is your sense of effectiveness, skill, and success when faced with the same scenario.

Powerlessness and strength are states of mind. No person is either, except as he believes it so. You develop a primary image of yourself as powerless or strong as a child, and reinforce it as an adult. However, given that you are dealing with a duality, you also develop the secondary trait. Your stopping point may be powerlessness, but you also possess strength, and that can be frightening. You may not sense it consciously, but your strength to go past all barriers is waiting to be set free, and you fear it.

Specifically, you wonder if your fear of strength—children feel responsible for all changes in their lives—coupled with the sense of powerlessness that you felt when your mother died, affected your life in your new family. The answer is yes. You felt that your only safe role was to obey every rule, no matter how it affected you, so that you would not harm more people. That attitude is virtually a prescription for unhappiness.

At the time of death or any major life change, it is essential that adults assure children that these changes have nothing to do with their actions. You were not given that reassurance, and you judged yourself harshly as a result.

RELATIONSHIPS ARE OFTEN BUILT ON THE POWERLESSNESS MODEL

Let us now examine powerlessness and strength in detail. We begin with powerlessness, because it is the most common fear reaction.

If you react passively when you feel powerless, you are likely to defer to the needs as well as the whims of others, because you believe their concerns are more important than yours. At the same time, you feel like a victim, and you often carry suppressed anger. You are indeed a victim of your thoughts.

If you react actively in the same scenario, you often insist on your own comfort at the expense of others. Because you believe that you have nothing of value to offer to another or to the world, you are likely to emphasize wants or whims over needs, to prove to yourself that you have dominance over at least one other person. However, your thoughts of unworthiness persist. Even though you have gotten your way now, what will happen next time?

Relationships often are based on active and passive versions of powerlessness. The dominant partner in such a relationship harbors suppressed anger and the sense of being a victim, because she carries the responsibility for all major decisions, as well as dealing with whatever changes occur. The subservient partner, in turn, harbors suppressed anger and the sense of being a victim for not being part of those choices.

If the dominant partner makes all the decisions and deals with change, that person operates from a position of strength.

If a judgment lies under this situation, the dominant partner has entered the fear-pair of powerlessness and strength, with powerlessness dominant. The judgment is often: *My partner is weak—and wrong—for putting me in the position of dealing with change.* It is a short step from there to self-questioning: *Will I fail, or perhaps die, because of this choice? What will others say or think of my choice?*

A person operating from an authentic sense of power may make the same decisions, but she makes them in a state of acceptance, which means making the best choice in each situation and letting it go. In fact, she will make better decisions, because they are not colored by judgments.

Why do people stay in a relationship built on the powerlessness model, if both people are angry and feel like victims?

They stay for the gifts. The subservient partner has a sense of safety that comes with giving the responsibility for all decisions regarding change to another. The dominant partner has a sense of strength that comes from power over another, while retaining the right to blame the passive partner for any problems that arise. In a family setting, this can lead to physical and mental abuse. In turn, the children of these unions often perpetuate the powerlessness model in their families.

The sense of union that is present in love cannot exist in the powerlessness-strength fear pair. Not only are you separate from the other in this fear-pair, you are also isolated from your own sense of self-worth.

FEAR OF STRENGTH GOES HAND-IN-HAND WITH FEAR OF POWERLESSNESS

The other side of this core fear-pair is fear of strength. Whether you play a subservient role or whether you are the dominant partner in a relationship built on the powerlessness and

97

strength fear-pair, assume that you fear your inner strength, in addition to feeling powerless.

The relationship teeters on a razor's edge. The dominant or subservient partner can put an end to it actively or passively, using solutions that range from violence to walking out. This shadow destroys any feeling of self-worth and confidence that may exist in either partner, because both fear the powerlessness inherent in this type of scenario.

The only way out is through acceptance, which allows one or both partners—ideally, both—to see their roles clearly.

What type of judgment gets a person into this type of relationship?

The judgment is: *I am not complete; I am lacking.* The lack can be physical—a sense of poverty is a driver for many marriages—but often it is mental, an inability to cope with one or more aspects of life-as-is: job issues, family situations, and loneliness are a few. If you go into a relationship with the feeling that the other person can heal an area of your life in which you feel inadequate, beware.

What about individual issues?

Consider the fear of heights. If you have such a fear, recognize that you have made a judgment along the lines of: *It is wrong to be this high, because I can die.* In truth, you do not panic over the change in elevation; what you really fear is the loss of control that you experience when you look down. At the same time, you contact a frightening sense of your strength. You have power over life and death; all you have to do is allow yourself to fall.

I assume there is a gift inherent in this fear of strength.

> The primary gift is your feeling of complete control over your world. You can make the decision to leave or stay in a relationship, or, in the case we just discussed, to live or die.

Fear of powerlessness is easier to visualize than fear of strength. How do we know the difference between the feeling that most of us have when we begin a job, project, or relationship—that something can and will go wrong—and the fear of powerlessness and strength that you are talking about?

> They are the same. You have made a judgment. At work, it could be: *This project could be valuable, but I know it will not succeed.* In your personal life, it could be: *This relationship is too good to be true; something will go wrong.* Fear of powerlessness and strength always follows a judgment, and it is usually a negative one.

But things can—and often do—go wrong, especially when we start something new.

> You have heard that there are no levels of fear. There is also no "time off," when judgments are expected and allowable. You have made a judgment and entered the realm of fear. Your only solution is to accept the fact that you have judged something as wrong or right, bad or good.

Let us envision a scenario. You have started a new project, as head of a community group that will prepare a report about the health of a local riparian area. Many things could go wrong: falsified data, not enough volunteers, inadequate equipment for testing, and the like. At the same time, what change are you afraid of if everything goes right? Will you prepare an excellent report, only to have no one read it or take it seriously? Will the area be lost despite your best efforts? On the other side of the coin, are you afraid that others will consider you an expert in this field? If so, how will your life change as a result?

Fear of strength is always present with fear of powerlessness. If you feel one, always look for its opposite. Once you have identified the source of your fear and the judgment behind it, you begin the process of acceptance and healing.

DID YOU GROW UP WITH AN IMAGE OF YOURSELF AS POWERLESS OR STRONG?

Some people seem to go through life fearing nothing, while others seem to be afraid of their shadows.

If you grew up with authoritarian dictates regarding how you used your time and energy, and no chance to explore your needs and wants without a sense of judgment hovering over you, you most likely carry an image of yourself as more powerless than strong. On the other hand, if you grew up knowing that your parents would defend your actions, no matter how they affected other people or other life, you carry an image of yourself as more strong than powerless, but at the expense of others.

In other words, a bully.

Yes. Both of these scenarios result in a person with a self-judgment of all-right or all-wrong, all-good or all-bad. Neither is a true picture. There is a third option. If you grew up in a family that respected your interests and feelings and gave you the time to explore them, and if you had the opportunity to find your own solutions without a sense of judgment if you erred, you carry an image of yourself as more strong than powerless, but in a positive way.

Recognize that when you grow up with a particular image of yourself, you have a tendency to react in predictable ways. For example, if you grew up with an image of powerlessness, you are probably inclined to be angry and to want to hide or run away, both figuratively and literally. Travel, books, music, sports, and the like can be used to escape from, rather than go toward, some end.

Other effects of the powerless image can be an unwillingness to bend to the needs and wants of others, with an accompanying sense of judgment; or a tendency to defer to others' needs when you do not want to do so, and subsequent anger.

How would a bully's life play out?

There are many similarities between these two versions of the powerlessness and strength scenario, because they are both based on judgments of all-good or all-bad, all-right or all-wrong. If you grew up with a false image of strength, you are also inclined to be angry, and to be unwilling to bend to the needs and wants of others, along with an accompanying sense of judgment.

It is easy to fall into the behavior of the controller when you grow up with this image, but it is also easy to fall into the behavior of the controller as victim. In other words, if you cannot get your way by being a bully, you may adopt the hairshirt of the martyr.

How about the third option, the child who grows up with a real image of strength, neither a bully nor a victim?

The biggest change would not be outward but inward, in a more centered sense of self, without anger and the desire to hide or escape that are present in the person with the powerless image, or anger and the desire to control that are present in the bully. That strong sense of self often enables people to bring their life purposes, the pathways in life that most suit them, to fruition early in life. The finest gift that parents can give children is to bring them up this way.

Is there any way people can escape this childhood conditioning?

You escape it by understanding it, then going beyond your conditioned limitations. For example, if you grew up with a powerless image, recognize that you tend to hide or escape, and that you are likely to deal with others' requests from a non-centered viewpoint, either as necessities that you must go out of your way to satisfy or as whims that you would not dream of accommodating. Then make other choices. If you grew up as a bully, recognize that you are likely to deal with others as people who must serve you, not as equals, and then make other choices.

Also, recognize that you fear your strength if you see yourself as powerless or as a bully. If you have a project to finish—that report on the wetland, for example—are you putting it off for any reason? Are you criticizing others, or blaming the issues or situations that the report itself brings up?

THE CORE FEAR-PAIR OF POWERLESSNESS AND STRENGTH AFFECTS EVERYONE

Can people who grow up with a balanced image of themselves avoid facing issues of powerlessness and strength?

Regardless of your self-portrait, you face the fear-pair of powerlessness and strength when you make a judgment. Additionally, once you enter the core fear-pair of powerlessness and strength for any reason, you will experience the other fear-pairs to a greater or lesser degree.

On a community level, what makes you feel powerless?

I feel frustrated as I watch business interests and highways gobble up the land. They are leaving no room for the reasons people came here: the sense of open space and the great gift of our native wildlife.

Often seemingly unfightable issues impinge on your day-to-day life. It is essential that you feel a sense of acceptance as you face them, so you can make a clear decision regarding your role.

Say you buy a new home, and a year later bulldozers begin to convert a nearby road into a freeway. What do you do?

While there are a number of ways that you can react in the powerlessness-strength fear-pair, a common response is to judge the situation and then subconsciously avoid making a decision. In other words, you feel you are at the mercy of the change that faces you, but at the same time you fear your strength: in this case, your ability to walk free, once you accept the change and make a choice regarding it.

If I judged the highway as good or right, I would not need to move, and I would not be fearful.

Although a positive judgment would seem to have little effect, the fear-pair would still be operative. Often home prices go down because of proximity to a highway, and houses are harder to sell. Those circumstances could be sources of fear.

Your only way out is through acceptance, because it opens you to all options. If you decide to leave, you are free to consider a home in a nearby neighborhood or on the other side of the country. If you decide to stay, you may call in a landscape specialist or general contractor to see what can be done to make your yard or home more resistant to noise and pollution; or you may spearhead a drive for a retaining wall that will deflect the noise from the highway.

On a societal level, you also face issues that impact your daily life. In the Southwest, people face growing water shortages as climate change accelerates. Communities in the East face the threat of hurricanes, Midwesterners face the danger of tornadoes, and towns and cities on the West Coast face the possibility of major earthquakes. The list goes on.

Given that these situations exist, what do you choose to do? Only with acceptance can you freely decide whether to stay in a particular area or leave. Additionally, only with acceptance can you freely choose what you will do to help the situation that you find yourself in: as part of a water conservation effort or as an advocate for reduced emissions to halt global warming, for just two examples.

Gandhi accepted British rule in India as a reality and decided on a role as activist. He challenged the most powerful nation on Earth and won freedom for his country. No issue or entity is so vast, so overpowering, that it cannot be confronted.

Understand, though, if you have grown up with a powerless image or the false bravado of the bully, these fears are going to feel bigger than they would if you had grown up with a true sense of strength.

WHAT ARE YOUR ISSUES REGARDING POWERLESSNESS AND STRENGTH?

Take a close look at your issues of powerlessness and strength.

Personal

In your personal life, do you feel powerless or strong? What are the dynamics behind your relationships with your parents, spouse, co-workers, friends, and children? Do your roles seesaw in these different relationships, or have they changed within one relationship over time? Are there ways to make your interactions more equitable?

Community, State, and Nation

Next, look at your role in your community, state, and nation. Every area faces issues of change. What do you choose to do to help resolve these issues? You can help in many ways, from writing letters to the editor or speaking up at meetings, to supporting or becoming active in organizations on the community, state, or national/international level. I recommend that everyone take on one or more community or societal issues that seem overwhelming. Give time, energy, money, or all three. It will empower you.

I urge you to write down your goals. The process of getting words on paper is an important one. Once the words are released, your mental liberation begins.

Chapter Seven

THE CORE FEAR-PAIRS OF SICKNESS AND HEALTH, AGING AND YOUTH

> You can simply elect to die, as
> did many of your Native
> American forebears. Most people
> choose sickness as the more
> conventional way to leave the
> body, but it is not necessary.
>
> Guardian of Water Clarification

Because we often associate sickness with aging, the fear-pairs of sickness and health, plus aging and youth, are considered together in this chapter. In fact, when the Guardian of Water Clarification asked me how I envisioned the aging process, I replied: "People get sick at all ages, of course, but as we grow older, our bodies grow less able to heal, and we die."

* * *

So, you believe that sickness precedes death.

Yes.

First, let us define some terms. Under the umbrella term *sickness*, let us include illness as

109

well as injury. Sickness, then, consists of all the conditions that define bad health, from the common cold to cancer, and from spraining your ankle to becoming a quadriplegic.

Under the umbrella term *health*, let us go beyond physical well-being to your sense of mental strength, vigor, and fitness. In truth, you may deem yourself strong and vital, although you have what others may consider a major health problem. The wheelchair-bound woman in your town who runs a thriving business feels that way.

Your comment was: "…our bodies grow less able to heal, and we die." Trust me when I tell you that God has no such plans for you. God did not create humanity with a built-in self-destruct program. Of course, if sickness is what you anticipate, it is what you will experience. You create your life. The truth is that people die when they are apparently in full health, and they die young.

The primary judgment behind these issues would seem to be that sickness is bad and health is good, but you fear the changes that both sickness and health can bring. Say you were terminally ill with cancer and suddenly had a full remission. Would your relationships with others—people who assumed you would die—be back to their old footing? What types of choices would you have to make concerning work, home, and family now that you face life, rather than death?

These vital issues in everyone's life are offshoots of the core fear-pair of powerlessness and strength. Both sickness and age engender a feeling of powerlessness, as you imagine a time that your body is no longer under your control. On the other side of the coin, you fear the strength that you may have to call on when you are sick or as you age: the courage to admit to yourself that it is time to die—or to live.

SICKNESS IS A CHOICE THAT IS REINFORCED BY BUSINESS AND POLITICAL INTERESTS

To avoid illness and injury, look to your mind. Always remember that when you live in any aspect of fear, your body patterns an outward expression that reflects the dominant focus of your mind.

In other words, if I live in fear, I can get sick.

You do not *get* sick, that implies an outside force. You *become* sick. It is your choice.

The process is straightforward: Once you enter the realm of fear through judgment, you can elect to fear illness or injury. And, such is the power of your mind that you often bring about that which you fear. Additionally, you can pattern a relationship on a sickness-health model. Many family members use sickness as a way to get special attention, while the healthy partner acts out the role of caregiver.

Illness or injury generally is a response to fear, and often a learned response. If family members have had heart disease or bone defects, for example, others in the family often believe that they will get them too. In some cases, they do, but you have also heard about people who carry this type of patterning and exhibit no symptoms.

Additionally, television and magazines carry many advertisements for drugs to help you overcome illness and maintain your vitality. The drug companies that sponsor these advertisements want you to believe that you are ill enough—or old enough—to buy their products.

Those ads are very expensive, and the drug companies are in business to make money, so what you say makes sense.

The pharmaceutical companies, and the sickness industry as a whole—the so-called health care industry is not health- but sickness-oriented—only get rich if you either believe that you are sick or think that your vitality is ebbing and you may become sick. What better way to achieve their goal than through focusing your mind on sickness?

The truth is that the sickness industry is a multi-billion-dollar behemoth that has outgrown its niche in society, so, like the great beasts of mythology, it searches for better sources of sustenance. The drug ads not only support pharmaceutical companies, they also support the industry as a whole. You see a physician because you think you need a specific drug. In response to your request, she may prescribe tests, or even recommend a short stay in the hospital.

Brief stays in the hospital are better than long ones, in terms of expense. In that way, at least, the health care—or sickness—industry is trying to help people.

If you were to check hospital ledgers, you would find that many short stays yield more revenue than fewer long ones. They also help individual insurance companies save money.

It sounds as if you are lumping all doctors, nurses, and hospital administrators into one big "bottom line" pile.

There are exceptions to every blanket statement, including many caring doctors, nurses, and administrators whose primary focus is healing. Witness also healers such as homeopaths, acupuncturists, and naturopaths, who do not benefit from the insurance that most Americans carry. However, when you look at the big picture, business interests control health care, from what drugs you take to insurance restrictions on the type of care you receive.

As large as the sickness industry looms, it represents only the tip of the iceberg. There are additional benefits to having a country filled with people who fear they are—or may become—sick. When your fear centers on your personal world, you are less likely to deal with the major issues that confront you, along with all life that shares the planet.

Industrial polluters are destroying air quality worldwide through noxious emissions. Chemical manufacturers have convinced farmers and individual homeowners to compromise the soil—and its great gift, the food that sustains life—through wholesale applications of herbicides, insecticides, and chemical fertilizers. Other manufacturers seek to overcome those excesses by genetically engineering plants and

113

animals so they will thrive—or at least grow—in this toxic mix. Similarly, the third great source of physical sustenance, water, is under attack by those who would contaminate it with impunity.

Where do you think this will end? Do you foresee a healthy society arising like a phoenix from wholesale pollution of the three building blocks of life: soil, air, and water?

Consider this: If you were a big polluter, whom would you choose for an enemy? Would you want to face a person whose mind is busy dealing with sickness or one who believes she is healthy? Accept the fact that businesses consider money, one of the three major gifts that the world offers, more important than your quality of life.

Similarly, your concentration on sickness is valuable to those who desire the world's second great gift, power. Who is riper for control, the person who is anxious about his personal health and well-being or the person who is free from the blinders of fear?

The world's third gift, fame, is a byproduct of the machinations of business and political interests for money and power. As such, it demonstrates your focus as a society. Who are your heroes? Humanitarians, such as Mother Theresa, who tended the desperately poor and ill? Politicians such as Lincoln, who freed the slaves; or Franklin Delano Roosevelt, who helped the downtrodden get on their feet? Inventors such as Edison?

Are you surprised that recent presidents have been primarily business-oriented, rather than long-range thinkers and humanitarians? Are you surprised that your community, in line with many, is increasingly dominated by chain stores and restaurants, rather than honoring the individual genius that you like to think of as American?

You use the term *real job* to describe work for another. Those words, often spoken jokingly, hide a truth: Personal industry is no longer revered in your society, unless an individual entrepreneur becomes wealthy—in effect, another big business owner.

What you have done as a people is to give your power away to business interests, which are increasingly allied with political interests. At the same time, you look to another big business—the sickness industry—to save you from the excesses of its brothers. In time, you will recognize that most occurrences of fatal illnesses such as cancer and heart disease, as well as a myriad number of chronic conditions such as diabetes and arthritis, can be traced directly or indirectly to the pollution caused by big businesses.

Your only way out is to take back your power, and you do that by stepping past fear. It is literally your way back to life.

But I really might be sick, and in that case, I would need to see a doctor. Are you advocating the end of all health care, insurance, and the like?

By all means, keep your insurance and see your doctor as necessary. What I advocate against is succumbing to the tactics that big business uses to drive you into fear. Therein lies your power.

MIND IS THE PRIMARY SOURCE OF SICKNESS

Do some people decide to be sick when they plan their lives in the astral world?

> Most souls choose healthy lives to accomplish their goals.

So, virtually all sickness starts on this plane.

> Yes.

What judgment do people make before they become sick?

> A judgment of bad is often the entryway to these fears, because you consider illness and injury as bad. However, some people elect to become sick for other reasons. They may consider a specific type of change in their lives bad and seek to control it by becoming dependent. You know of a family in which the mother became chronically ill after her adult children left home, and now one of them cares for her.

What about people who were exposed to environmental toxins and to carcinogens such as Agent Orange in Vietnam? Surely they are not responsible for the illnesses that result from those chemicals.

> Anyone who is exposed to chemicals is called to a higher level of response: the choice not to be ill. In Vietnam, a number of service people were not affected adversely, although they were exposed to Agent Orange. The secret lies in their power of belief.

This is a hard theory to swallow. I can understand what you are saying about illness that is theoretically under my control—if a family member has cancer, I may believe I will get it too—but not something like this.

This is a tough concept, but it is a core truth of your existence. By all means, eat organic vegetables and naturally grown poultry, fish, and meat, in order to limit your exposure to these toxic chemicals; and do visit doctors as necessary. Some sicknesses are genetically based; however, in most instances you are the arbitrator of sickness or health, in yourself and ultimately the Earth.

People with multiple personalities demonstrate my point. One personality might be myopic, while her alter-ego is farsighted; another may have severe back pain, while his alter-ego is the perfect picture of health. Both of these conditions exist in the same person; their presence or absence depends totally on the power of belief of the personality in control.

Are minor illnesses, such as the flu or colds, fear reactions too?

I mentioned a situation in which a mother chose chronic illness in order to control the challenges of change as her sons and daughters left home. You choose minor illnesses and injuries for a variant of the same reason. While colds or strained muscles do not transform your overall life pattern, they do give you time to unwind for a day or two. What better time to assess the impact of change and its accompanying stress?

What is the judgment underlying these conditions?

> In virtually all cases, the judgment is: *This change is bad.*

If I understand your messages correctly, the judgment can also be: *This change is good.*

> That is true. A judgment of good opens the way to fear as effectively as a judgment of bad, because the opposite always lurks in your mind.
>
> In situations such as health and sickness, however, consider the negative judgment to be stronger than the positive one. In other words, you are primed to be sick, and much of your belief is based in the tactics of big business that we discussed.

What about allergies?

> Generally, an allergy is the body's demonstration to the mind that it functions optimally when it is shielded from certain food or chemical stressors. Unless you have developed an allergy because you expect to do so—others in your family have it, for example—it can be a valuable warning system.

ON A WIDER SCALE, SICKNESS CAN BEGIN IN THE MIND OF EARTH

> Remember that illnesses and injuries are always present for a reason, and the reason is as individual as the person. So far, we have

118

considered only the judgments behind sickness; we also need to discuss the lessons that sickness can teach.

I want to ask a question before we go on to that topic. Why do the viruses and bacteria that cause illness exist at all?

The answer is found in nature herself, in her checks and balances. Viruses and bacteria are not necessarily bad; they are cleansing.

The Earth's goal is to rid itself of impurities. When any species gets too large for the Earth to support, or if that species is the cause of dis-ease—disruption and disorder, rather than illness or injury *per se*—in the interrelated web of life forms, the planet utilizes bacteria and viruses to cleanse itself.

Will we see more and more of this type of cleansing, given the growing number of people and our ongoing damage to the environment?

Unless you begin to limit your numbers voluntarily, the Earth will regulate them. This purification, of course, will help take care of the environment; fewer people equal less pollution.

So, in effect, we may not be making the decision to be ill. The Earth may be doing that for us.

Assume that you are making the decision. The truth is that even if the Earth does begin a cleansing process, illness is always your choice. Generally, when a disease cycle begins, people become afraid, and their fear opens them to the infection. In that sense, the planet does not purify itself; the species cleanses itself through fear.

What about the meteor explosions that wiped out much life on the planet? Are you saying that the dinosaurs did not have to die?

> Yes. Their fear killed them. You could survive a nuclear explosion at ground zero, if you so willed.
>
> Assume that everything the great masters could do, you can do as well. It is in you. It may not be dominant because of your fear, but you have the capacity of Jesus of Nazareth, Buddha, or Krishna.

BEGIN THE PROCESS OF HEALING

This discussion makes me feel as if I am a failure if I become sick.

> This brings us to the teaching aspects of sickness. You certainly can blame yourself; that is one reaction. Ultimately, though, each illness or injury can be your teacher. You can heal your mind and your body by honoring your sickness for the truth that is behind it. As we have discussed, in most cases you are dealing with what is in effect a bodily demonstration of internal fear.
>
> First, thank your fear that expresses as illness or injury. It has taken you to your doorway in the eye of the rainbow; without it, you might not know how much fear is seething within you. Fear is not the absence of, but the shutting out of, love. It is a door that you close, and that you can learn to open.

Next, ask what is to be learned from your sickness. If you sit in concentrated prayer or meditation to open your mind, and then ask in silence, you can become aware of its teachings. Your answer may come in a dream, an intuitional understanding, a book that you pick up, even a comment from a friend. If you do not get an answer, keep asking.

Once you receive an answer that feels right, work back to the judgment that underlies it. The judgment could be anything from: *This sickness is good, because my family has to care for me now*; to *this sickness is bad, but I knew I was going to get it, because it is increasingly widespread.* Do you see the choice for sickness under both judgments?

This process often restores you to health, because sickness begins and ends in the mind. It only exhibits in the body. As with any fear, once you unmask it, it begins to dissipate.

What about people who take on the illnesses of others? I have heard of such people.

Leave that work to the saints! Assume that your sickness is internally generated and has to do entirely with you, no one else.

FEAR OF HEALTH ACCOMPANIES FEAR OF ILLNESS OR INJURY

After you thank your fear expressed as illness or injury and find out its teachings, ask what is to be learned about your fear of health. Do you fear *not* catching a family illness? Remember how strong the gift of walking in step with others of your kind is. Do you fear an upcoming situation so strongly that you would rather be sick than go through it? Do you dislike a responsibility—your job, family obligations, or the like—enough to wish that you did not have deal with it?

What I am saying is that illness or injury can serve as an answer to an unspoken prayer. In effect, you fear health.

Your mind is indeed a devious friend! However, remember that it is always a friend, in that it always seeks the best for you and wishes to protect you. That is why you must thank your fears and ask what they would teach; they all begin—and end—in your mind.

WHAT ARE YOUR ISSUES REGARDING SICKNESS AND HEALTH?

Overall, do you feel sick or healthy most of the time?

Family Influences

What types of illnesses or injuries have you had during the past few years? Are they similar or identical to those that family members have experienced, or do they echo those that you experienced in childhood?

Your Reaction to Sickness

How do you deal with sickness? Do people tend to ignore you or cater to you when you are sick? Do you, or others that you know, use sickness to achieve certain ends? If you find yourself predisposed to choose sickness, remember that you can always choose again.

Your Attitude Toward Health

Similarly, what is your attitude toward health? Is being healthy a burden sometimes? Are there at present, or were there in the past, situations in which you chose to be sick, rather than deal with them? Do you fear *not* catching a family illness?

Have you recovered from a life threatening illness or injury only to feel that your family and friends expected you to die, and readjusted their lives accordingly?

Your goal is to choose and welcome health. It is your birthright.

THE PROCESS OF AGING DOES NOT HAVE TO BE FEARFUL

We turn to fear of aging next. As with your fears of sickness and health, it begins with a judgment. Most often, you interiorize aging as bad.

Aging is different from sickness, in that it is a natural process. Much of your fear of aging is based on false societal norms. At one point in your existence, people lived two to three hundred years. The only difference between you and them is that you do not expect to live that long.

I read of a woman in France who reached one hundred and twenty, and even that age seems impossible.

I tell you this: As a society, you do not want to age. Once you begin to revere age, individuals in your society can—and will—live vitally to two hundred and beyond. The human body is capable of long life; the human mind shortens its span.

Why do we choose shorter lives?

In brief, you do not want to face two of the four exquisite stages of life. Just as each year contains four seasons, so does your life, and that of your nation. The softness of spring gives way to the intensity of summer, which, in turn, opens the doorway to autumn's fullness and winter's strength. Each season has its place, its job to perform.

You as a nation fear age because, as individuals, you fear the aging process. Conversely, you worship youth because that is how you want to perceive yourselves. You still secretly admire your days of taming the West, although you now conquer it in land yachts rather than Conestoga wagons. As a nation and as individuals, you fear autumn and winter; thus, you turn your faces toward spring and summer.

Consider the attributes of spring in a young man or woman's life. The time from birth through the mid-twenties is marked by physical prowess and vibrancy, by regularity of form and feature, and by a sense of abandon that comes when you see an unlimited span of years before you. In spring, you cannot visualize harvest.

Summer, the ages of twenty-four through forty-five in your current belief system of one hundred years, is a time of ripening, flowering, and setting fruit. It is the season of your drive toward perfection. In summer, you bring up children and pursue careers. Summer is marked by physical competence and grace, and by beauty of form. You begin to think of harvest and winter, but only momentarily. Your lives are filled with doing and getting.

In comparison with spring, autumn has an idiosyncratic beauty, which comes from experiencing life. It still is characterized by loveliness of form, but the form is fuller and there is intelligence in the eyes. It still is distinguished by vibrancy, but it is a *joie de vivre* accented and honed by an awareness of winter. The sense of abandon gives way to deliberate action, and the self-centeredness of youth yields to a consciousness of the needs of others. It is altogether a more likeable state of mental development than spring or summer.

Nations, as well as individuals, age. As a nation, you are now at the threshold of autumn. My hope is that you acknowledge your age. If you live your autumn well, you can look forward to a vital winter, not the cartoon of old age—both of countries and people—that you currently favor, a product of your fear.

In an ideal life, winter has as much fight, and as much depth of being, as the season. Your concept of putting people out to pasture just as they reach a degree of wisdom is shortsighted. It is not only demeaning to them; it is also destructive to society. There are many ways that those in the winter season can assist a country that does not equate age with infirmity or senility. As a nation and as individuals, you look at winter from the callow perspective of early spring: a teenage outlook, if you will.

Winter is a time of heightened consciousness of self and others. The real beauty of winter is in the eyes, which have lived long enough to attain sagacity and inner strength. In the body, it is a time of dignity and poise.

People dodder and become sick because society, and hence they, expect it. You can live your winter with great passion, determination, and strength of will. This includes the insight that ultimately determines when and how you will die. Witness your heroes: Georgia O'Keeffe, the painter who defined the silence of the West and the inner lives of flowers; and Marjorie Douglas, the writer who rescued the Everglades. Not only did they live their winter season fully; they also knew when it was time to depart this life, and they died with a sense of completion. That awareness, acceptance, and choice regarding death are the gifts of a vibrant winter season.

The aging process is inevitable. You have a choice, as individuals and as a nation, for adventure and wisdom, or for a rocking chair and planned obsolescence.

But our bodies do grow more fragile as we age.

If you are alert and responsive to your body's inner intelligence, you can have a healthy, vigorous winter season. Your body processes change, and you must support those changes. You need less, and better, food. You require less strenuous, but longer-lasting, periods of exercise.

Most important, your mind demands a passion, a reason to stay alive. Vitality follows as night follows day, when you direct the wisdom of age toward a goal such as expansion of mind or spirit, or service to humanity or other life.

The wisdom of staying in charge of your mental powers is obvious. I use the term *mental powers* to mean your connection with the world outside the inner world of your mind. As they age, many people progressively retreat inside their minds until they live there entirely. They do so because of fear, tiredness, and ultimately a longing for death. The mind becomes increasingly confused when it is necessary to make contact with the world outside its borders, and eventually it no longer does so.

There can be physical reasons for this change, but for most it is primarily a decision, a choice. It is also an easy trap to fall into, because of your society's view of age.

In sum, winter is more about the mind than the body, just as spring is more about the body than the mind. I add that if you believe that birth, not death, follows life in this dimension—that you are simply born to another existence—you are guaranteed a happier, calmer winter season.

I tell you something else: The gift of old age, the winter that I speak about, begins at eighty in your current belief system of one hundred years. I remind you again that this is a belief system that not all share. If you expect to live until your mid-hundreds, or even two hundred, you can do so. In that case, old age begins approximately twenty years before you plan to die.

The challenge of autumn and winter is to develop mental agility in place of physical dexterity. With insight, you know why you are injured or ill, and the lessons behind the sickness. You also know when it is time to die to your present existence. This is a big order, I admit, but it is the directive—and the direction—of age.

Your goal, individually and as a nation, is wisdom. My greatest wish is that you become true winter flowers. Only with nations of seers—wise men and women—will the Earth survive.

WE FEAR YOUTH AS WELL AS AGE

Accept your fear of age, and ask what it would teach you; then do the same with your fear of youth. Understand that beneath your earnest striving for the physical perfection of youth is fear of that time of life.

Are there parts of your life that you would rather not relive? Did you have a childhood that was marked by powerlessness, which transformed in adulthood into demanding too much of others or becoming too subservient? Did you chase success to the exclusion of your family? Would you have gone into a different line of work?

The key is acceptance. Accept what you did and why you did it. Then, ask what you learned by living as you did, and listen for answers.

Additionally, if you would revise a particular life experience, revisit it in silence and do so. For example, if you were ashamed of your family because your parents drank to excess, return to that memory and picture them as sober and happy. If you hated your incompetence on the soccer field, go back to that memory and experience yourself as a winner.

Of course, you will not change a particular event; it happened as it did. However, by reliving it in that way, you come closer to inner peace. In effect, you revise your life portrait.

What good does that do? The past is still the past.

Once you change your life portrait—your mind's image of yourself—you begin the process of change in your outer life. Here is another example. A man may have a fear of public speaking because of a negative experience in high school, when friends belittled his attempts on the debate team. Once he revisits that experience and revises it to a positive ending, he begins to heal the fear.

The subconscious mind stores memories both on the dream or visionary level and on the conscious or outer level, and it does not distinguish between them. Thus, you store an alternative memory pattern when you revisit painful memories. In effect, you heal your life.

WHAT ARE YOUR ISSUES REGARDING AGING AND YOUTH?

Think of two older people, living or dead, who inspire you. How did they live their winter season? What are their teachings for you?

129

What Are Your Choices for an Expanded Lifespan?

If you could live a long as you want, what age would you choose to die? What would you like to accomplish in your autumn and winter years?

What Would You Change?

Would you be young again, if you could choose that option? What experiences and situations in your life would you revise?

Your goal is to go past the point of view of your society in this vital matter and decide what is best for you. You can have a life similar to Merlin's (chapter 2), including an extended lifespan and a conscious exit from the body, if you so choose.

Chapter Eight

THE CORE FEAR-PAIRS OF LACK AND ABUNDANCE, FAILURE AND SUCCESS

Humanity equates the intangible
energy of money, power, and
fame with vastness—or, more
accurately, with bigness. What
you must remember is that love
is the king of energies, the
crown. You worship a belt
instead of a diadem, but you will
learn in time.

Guardian of Communication

At some point in our lives, most of us face fears associated with abundance and lack, and success and failure. These fears bring up the questions: How much do I need to have a feeling of abundance? What makes me feel like a success?

This series of communications began with a refrain that may sound familiar. I complained on paper: "My income is too low. I need some more clients."

* * *

ABUNDANCE: COMFORT WITH LIFE AS-IS

You may *desire* more income, but you *need* a sense of abundance and success.

We begin with a definition. *Abundance* is your sense of comfort when you know that you have the physical, mental, and emotional well-being for a full expression of life.

Notice that I do not say that you have to be rich, in excellent health, or smart to have a sense of abundance. The key is your belief that you can live your dreams, which include achieving career goals, caring for your family, traveling, and the like. With a sense of abundance, you also have a surplus, in the form of money, material possessions, time, or energy to give to others.

Abundance, then, does not rely primarily on outer conditions. The man who cuts lawns and lives in a small apartment above the thrift store and the woman who owns a thriving business and lives in the restored Victorian that dominates Main Street have a comparable sense of abundance.

They belong to the same church, so we will use that as a point of reference. He gives only a small stipend, but he volunteers to cut and rake the church lawn weekly. She provides much of the capital to keep the building in good repair. Both gifts are equal, because both people have the continued well-being of the church as their goal. You tend to see money as more important than time or energy, but it is not so.

I add that although abundance is primarily a mental state, you need enough in the way of material possessions to feel comfortable. Beyond these essentials, however, the differences are superficial. Both the man and the woman have a comfortable place to live, good food, adequate transportation, and necessary income for electricity, telephone, heat, and the like. Additionally, both have adequate tools and resources to do their work. He stores his lawn mower, rake, and snow shovel in a shed; she has an ornate room set aside as a home office and an executive suite at her place of business.

Moreover, both have what they consider satisfactory physical and mental health. She is disabled, but that does not impair her business acumen. He is full of vitality and knows much about the growing habits of plants after a previous lifetime as a farmer. Most importantly, he and she believe their work is significant, to themselves as well as to others, and both give of what they have.

Notice that I have not said much about money. If the woman had a Ford rather than a Mercedes, and a cabin rather than an expansive home, she could—and would—run her business. Physical comfort derives from your sense of rightness, wherever in life you are situated. When you use your time and energy to achieve your life purpose, your physical, mental, and emotional health are synchronous with that sense of rightness, and giving to others is its outer expression.

Your society places great importance on money, power, and fame, but your time and energy are your lasting gifts. Your focused time and energy may result in prosperity, the ability to control other lives, and prominence in your community or the world, but these rewards are not promises, nor are they permanent.

Of two people doing the same work, one may be rich, famous, and influential, while the other lives and works in obscurity. To cite just one example, Paul Gauguin, whose paintings are sought by museums and collectors worldwide, was poor and virtually unknown in his lifetime, eclipsed by artists whose names are no longer remembered.

Additionally, money, power, and fame tend to be cyclical; you may be poor in one part of your life and wealthy in another, or famous as a child and a has-been at twenty. Most importantly, when you die, you are required to give up these gifts, which your society deems so vital.

Does that mean I keep my gifts of time and energy after I die?

In effect, you do retain them, because you evaluate your life based on how well you used them to achieve your life purpose, and you plan your next life based on that evaluation. We have spoken about the after-death evaluation (chapter 2), and we will discuss your life purpose further when we talk about success and failure.

If I have a life purpose, then I have a life story before I am born.

Indeed. In the astral realm, you preplan your lifespan on Earth to accomplish your primary goals. Of course, just as an architect cannot foresee all uses for a building, you cannot plan your life in its entirety while you are on the astral plane. However, you do put into place a blueprint—or, I should say that many do so. Some simply know that they want to be born as humans, and they make no specific plans. Their time on Earth may be spent finding out what their astral blueprint for the next life should look like. There are no hard and fast rules.

FEAR OF ABUNDANCE

This is a fear-pair, so it must follow that I fear abundance. Why would I be scared of something that is good?

To answer this question, we need to back up a bit. Throughout your lifetime, you judge yourself, based on your life portrait (chapter 4). Particularly if you carry an image of yourself as bad or your ideas as wrong, you may decide that you are unworthy to enjoy a comfortable life and achieve your goals.

You often develop this negative self-portrait because others seek to depend on you. They live on the powerless side of the powerlessness-strength fear-pair and expect you to augment their sense of strength. You cannot do that; not even Jesus of Nazareth could do so.

Do parents do this type of thing to their children, or is this an adult-to-adult issue, say, a wife who wants to depend on her husband?

It can be both, but it primarily begins in childhood, with parents who give up their roles. They may subject their children to inappropriate emotional outbursts, demand that a son take care of physical tasks around the home that more appropriately belong to them, or require a daughter to provide the primary emotional support for a sick or aging relative.

These are situations in which children cannot expect to have a feeling of satisfaction or completion, because they are beyond their capacity. Being chastised by a parent for not fulfilling an impossible role is often the source of a negative self-image.

Whatever the cause, if you find a self-judgment of bad or wrong in your childhood life portrait, it is easy to allow others to steal your time and energy as an adult. When that happens, you judge them as you judge yourself: as bad or wrong. Then you become angry: at the others for stealing your time and energy, and at yourself for allowing it to happen. It is an endless circle.

It is but a short step to the belief that once you get something of value, others will appropriate it. The safest way to live with this mindset is to deny yourself anything that another person can steal. You may ask for abundance, but fear it too much to allow it into your life. You also may decide not to live dreams that are important to you. In other words, you feel safest denying yourself the fruits of abundance.

What is the way past this type of fear?

First, acknowledge and accept the fact that you fear abundance. Then try to find its roots in your past. Did a parent, another authority figure, or a sibling usurp your time, energy, or possessions? Next, visualize the worst outcome.

136

What would happen if someone were to steal everything you have worked for? How would he do it? What would your life be like? Finally, visualize the best outcome. Substitute a new memory pattern for a past event or a future scenario.

In addition, understand that you compensate by acting out fear behaviors. You may deflect your fear by being angry with another, you may believe that by working fifteen hours a day you can avoid being afraid, or you may retreat to a more comfortable "home" in the past or the future. We will address fear behaviors in detail shortly.

Seeing your fear clearly is your first step to replacing its force with another way of looking at the world.

LACK: BELIEF THAT THERE IS NOT ENOUGH

Belief in lack differs from fear of abundance, although the consequences are often the same. I define *lack* as your belief that there is not enough physically, mentally, and emotionally. Note that I use the word *and*; when you feel lack in one area, you feel it to some degree in all. The core belief behind lack is a sense of scarcity. There is just so much money, there are just so many jobs, and even love has its limits. When you live in the state of lack, there is little or nothing left over to give to others. No matter how much you actually possess, you must hold onto what you have. A millionaire can have a feeling of lack and a poor person can have a sense of abundance.

Why would a wealthy person, in effect, feel like a pauper?

Similarly to the person who fears abundance, the person who believes that lack is predominant often is the victim of a negative life portrait from childhood. Moreover, she may have had parents who believed there was never enough, or who squandered money. I would advise such a person to look at her life portrait. Why is it frightening to live an expansive life?

FEAR OF LACK

If you believe in lack, that there is never enough of anything, it follows that you live in fear of lack, particularly concerning society's gifts of money, power, and fame. To a degree, this fear is justified; society's gifts often are bestowed arbitrarily and withdrawn capriciously.

To overcome the fear of lack, you use an approach similar to that of fear of abundance. Most important, consider any financial difficulties that you face to be illusions, ephemeral and without substance. I label them illusions, because your judgments of good and bad, right and wrong power your experiences. A millionaire would deem herself a pauper if her savings account dwindled to $10,000, while a pauper would consider himself rich with the same amount of money. Who is correct?

In the face of any fear, it is vital to look at it clearly and uncover the thought-creation behind it. For example, if you worry about money today, and receive $50,000 or $500,000 tomorrow, has your fear of lack not vanished, at least for the moment?

However, if you do not confront your thought-creation, you will superimpose another aspect of the same fear on this windfall, perhaps concern over the tax payment you must make. Alternatively, you may lose your newfound wealth at a gaming table, in a risky investment, in drugs or alcohol, or in the desire for more possessions. You may even give it away because you do not believe that you deserve it. You have read about lottery winners who have done all of these things.

Replacing the fear-thought is the only way to achieve stability. You do that by isolating the particular thought-creation—in this case, fear of lack—and accepting it.

You do not avoid the fear; you confront it by acknowledging its existence in your mind. As you did with fear of abundance, try to find its roots in your past. Then, envision the worst that could happen if your fear were brought to its conclusion. Fear of lack does not deal only with your bank account; you also may visualize losing your shelter, transportation, and relationships with family or friends. Finally, revisit and revise your fear scenario with one of joy and abundance. Picture yourself writing out checks for people and causes that are important to you, for example.

Once you expose fear to the light of understanding, it begins to dissipate, either fully or partially. It is no longer hidden and unexpressed.

WHAT ARE YOUR ISSUES REGARDING LACK AND ABUNDANCE?

For your peace of mind, it is important that you address the pervasive fears of lack and abundance.

Specific Issues

In which areas of your life do you feel a sense of abundance? Go beyond possessions. For example, do you feel rich in friendships, health, or in a comfortable working environment?

Similarly, in what areas of your life do you feel a sense of lack? Again, go beyond money to intangibles.

Steps to Freedom

What are your worst- and best-case scenarios regarding the specter of lack? Are there practical steps that you can take to forestall your worst-case scenario and achieve your best-case scenario?

Do you give of your time, energy, or money? This is an empowering and freeing step.

SUCCESS AND FAILURE DEFINED

We turn next to success and failure, which differ from the fear-pair of abundance and lack in that they are dependent on whether you pursue your life purpose. You consider yourself a success and live with a sense of abundance when you live the life that best suits you, and you consider yourself a failure and live in a state of lack when you do not do so.

Note that I have made no mention of society's gifts. You can feel like a failure even if you are rich, powerful, and famous. Your heart knows, even if your society does not. It is *that* essential.

ACCESSING YOUR LIFE PURPOSE

You said that we plan our lives on the astral level. It is one thing to plan a life purpose, but quite another to put it into effect. Few of us remember those plans.

The only way you can get in touch with your life purpose is through silence. Stop your activities for an instant or an hour, to steep yourself in stillness of mind and body. Silence is the source of your strength, not activity: the work you do all day, the thinking and planning. In the end, only the creative ideas that are born in stillness survive.

As you sit in silence, decide what you want—perhaps a clear picture of your personal or professional life purpose, or a new life purpose when you make a major life transition, such as retirement. Then decide how to find the answers you need. If, as most people do, you trust your mind as the arbiter of your way, you may choose to look in your local library or bookstore for an appropriate book, or resolve to see a career counselor.

I recommend that you also listen for intuitive guidance. This guidance may come visually, in the form of a dream that contains a view of your life as it can be, or that symbolically points the way to your life-to-be. It also may come in the form of an idea for a direction, or a sense of rightness when you consider a certain pathway. It may come as ideas that you translate into words on paper, or by way of a comment from a friend; a newspaper, magazine, or Internet article; or a book. Act on faith that you will have an answer.

How long does this process take?

Your answer may come in an hour, a day, a week, or a year, depending on your degree of receptivity. If you are not ready to receive answers, you will not get them. You may not be willing to consider any changes in your life-as-is, you may be afraid to get an answer that points you in a different direction than the one you are already committed to, or you may be skeptical of the whole process.

Assuming that I get an answer, how do I know that it is the right one?

In whatever way you receive your answer, I advise you to live with it for a month or longer. If you feel comfortable praying, ask for guidance. Your confirmation will come as a growing sense of rightness as you live with, and expand on, your plan day by day. Also, once you place your focus on your life purpose, doors open in unexpected ways. Simply be alert and aware.

Be aware also that your plans may change during different stages of your life. For example, you may study to become an engineer, and later use that skill to help archaeologists reconstruct an ancient city; or you may work as an accountant during your business years and decide to become a hospice volunteer after retirement.

If you have come to a point at which you sense there should be a change, ask for your truth at this stage. Many people walk diverse paths. For example, the spiritual teacher Joel Goldsmith started out as a businessman, and the poet Wallace Stevens was a banker.

Remember that all paths have as their goal a full expression of love: of yourself, of others of your kind and other life, and ultimately of God. Finding your life purpose is your highest expression of love of self. This love, in turn, leads you to your highest expression of love of others, up to and including God.

Should everyone do this kind of self-analysis, even people who have a direction?

It is a good idea to ask for confirmation that you are on your best path. Again, ask for what you would have and expect an answer. You may become aware of more rewarding or simpler ways to achieve your life purpose.

THE GIFTS OF THE WORLD OFTEN ARE BASED IN FEAR

What about people who grab money, power, or fame whatever way they can: corporate raiders, for example? Some people do not worry about life purposes, and they certainly seem to enjoy the world's gifts.

Their goal is outer achievement, not what they most desire to do in life.

The three gifts of the world—power, fame, and money—often have fear as their foundation. If you believe that you have to compete with others for the best idea to resolve an issue, the swiftest way to accumulate money, or the key to the executive suite, be assured that you operate from a sense of separateness, not union, and specifically from the fear-pair of lack and abundance, along with its companions, success and failure. Because the focus on competition for these gifts is so widespread, it is hard to see them as the fear-constructs that they are.

Additionally, remember that power, fame, and money are transient. Few people, including the richest, the most famous, and the most powerful, are remembered ten years after their deaths, and only a handful are kept alive in history books. As we have discussed, even within a lifetime, these gifts can be fleeting. How many people are poor in one part of their lives and rich in another, or famous and powerful, only to become has-beens, the subject of jokes?

If these gifts are based in fear, then there has to be a judgment behind them.

Yes. The judgment is always: *There is not enough.* Even the most ferocious corporate raider fears lack at some level.

So, is the secret to being happy not to seek the world's gifts?

The secret to being happy is not to make them your life purpose. If they come as part of what you do, they are in their proper place. Edison, for example, focused on harnessing electricity, not on the money and fame he would have as a result. Ford concentrated on making cars for the masses, not on the huge industry that he would spearhead. Certainly both men thought about the gifts of success, but those gifts were not their primary objectives.

Do not fear money, power, and fame. Simply do not place them in first in your thinking. In fact, when you do not do so, they flow naturally and easily into your life. You may or may not be the richest or most famous or powerful person on the planet, but you will always have enough to complete what you set out to do, and to give to others.

FEAR OF SUCCESS IS AS COMMON AS FEAR OF FAILURE

The inner feeling of accomplishment that marks you as a success also is frightening. In fact, fear of success is as pervasive as fear of failure.

Why would I be afraid of success?

Think of your life purpose as a fork in the road—a path that you can take, or not. Often people decide not to leave a known, safe path, simply because the alternative looks harder than the one they are on. In actuality, not following the path of your heart is the most dangerous way to walk, because it deadens your inner vision. You stray far from your individual truth.

What is it you want to be and do in life? Would you be a corporate lawyer, or Thor Heyerdahl building the raft *Kon Tiki* to sail across the Pacific? Either choice has its drawbacks as well as its rewards; however, if you would be Heyerdahl, understand that the further from the world's gifts you walk, the more suspect you are in many—if not most—people's minds. Adventurers such as Heyerdahl are respected only after they reach their goals, and only if those aspirations result in fame, fortune, and power.

The larger reality, however, is that if you use your time and energy to bring a life purpose into being, whether it is as a corporate lawyer, an explorer such as Heyerdahl, an industrial innovator such as Ford, an inventor such as Edison, or the man who cuts lawns, you are a success.

In what ways do we subvert our life purposes?

You can sabotage your inner truth consciously, by discarding it as impractical, and making money, power, and fame your goals. You can also undermine it subconsciously, by refusing to acknowledge its existence.

You are saying that in our hearts, we all know what path is best for us.

Yes. There can be many reasons behind your choice to block this inner truth. You may prefer to live off the energy generated by the concern of others, rather than being your own dynamo. In other words, you may choose to live as a victim. You also may consider it too risky, or, on the other side of the coin, see it as tame and unimportant.

How many people are strong enough to go past job titles and salaries as determiners of the significance of what they do in life? The man or woman whose heart-truth lies in the running of a junkyard is a recycler whose work could be more important in its effect on society, and to the land, than any white collar or managerial position. There is no distinction in any life purpose—the way of living and being that is best for you.

Without the sense of being in the right place in life, you waste your life. The individual who lives his dream as a junkyard owner has the possibility of more inner growth and happiness than the corporation president who has money and power as her goals.

What of those who must work long hours each day just to survive? I think of the people who do piecework in sweatshops.

The rule still exists, even for them. It is easier for you, who have more, to see your way; in fact, that makes your responsibility for opening to your truth greater.

Here is the crux. You have the freedom to ignore or accept your life purposes, but in actuality, you must pay a high price when you turn away. Setting your dreams aside often results in health problems, diminished sexual capacity and interest, and an overall dissociation from the pain as well as the pleasure and richness of life. You live a diminished life.

Paradoxically, following the dictates of your heart, an action that often is dismissed as self-seeking and self-centered, most helps others. For example, in following their dream of providing high quality organic foods, nearby farm owners help themselves financially while they restore and sustain the health of a wide community. They raise the quality of life in the area.

Life purposes can be small or large in scope, but they are always large in effect. The man who cuts lawns improves the lives of those that live in your town by beautifying it. The woman business owner improves the lives of those whom she employs by providing them with work, as well as a way to house, clothe, and feed their families.

How about the people who work for her? Are they following their life purposes?

They certainly can be doing so. The answer is as individual as the person. For the man with a life purpose of using his mechanical skills, a job at her factory may be the right answer.

Anyone who follows a life purpose is a success, and success ripples outward like the ever-widening circles that mark the spot where a pebble is tossed into a still pond. Many are inspired to follow their dreams in response to the joy and completion that they sense in this person.

Some people consider you a fool if you follow your dreams.

Remember the dictum that you can never please all of the people all of the time. Not even Francis of Assisi was loved universally. Any strongly held goal inspires strong passions, both pro and con. Expect both extremes; do not be surprised.

WHAT ARE YOUR ISSUES REGARDING FAILURE AND SUCCESS?

Take a hard look at your attitude toward failure and success.

Priorities

How important are the gifts of money, fame, and power to you, and what are you willing to do to get them? Are you willing to live your life purpose, and allow these gifts to flow in as they will?

Self-Assessment

In what areas of your life do you feel like a failure, and in what areas do you feel like a success?

What are your worst- and best-case scenarios? Are there practical steps that you can take to avoid the worst-case scenarios and achieve the best-case scenarios?

WHAT WOULD YOUR IDEAL LIFE LOOK LIKE?

Visualize how you would live if you had unlimited abundance, health, energy, and time. Are you living the life that is most in harmony with your dreams, or is there more that you would like to do? Are there goals you would like to achieve in this phase of your life, or after retirement? Would you travel around the world, play chess professionally, own your own business, or buy a car that has been a dream for many years?

I urge you to write down your dreams, then pick the one that is most important to you. Divide it into short- and long-term goals, along with the steps you need to take to bring each goal to life. After that, follow through. It will empower and expand you.

ANY MAJOR CHANGE CAN BE CONSIDERED A MINI-DEATH

Although we speak of physical death here, every major life change contains some of the elements that we are discussing. You are often forced to let go of people, places, things, and ideas when you confront a major life change. In that sense, it can be considered a mini-death.

For example, when you marry or make a significant career move, your relationships with family and friends are transformed, along with your usual ways of living. Some of these adjustments may seem big and others small, but all are important. You are, in effect, modifying your life portrait.

You burden change—including death—with judgment and fear, because you are afraid of facing the unknown. To be happy, you must be present *now* and accept all, the seemingly good as well as the seemingly bad. I say *seemingly*, because your opinion often becomes modified after you live with change for a while. This includes the change marked by death.

Do we primarily make subconscious choices when we are confronted by change, the same as we do regarding death?

Yes. We use a career move as an example. There are many questions associated with this change, including: How will this choice affect your relationships with friends and family? What will you have to leave behind, and what will you gain? For the most part, people deal with the outer aspects of the change, such as buying a home and calling in movers, but they bury the emotional issues. These unanswered questions are a big part of the fear of change.

With awareness and acceptance of all the aspects of any change, you make a truly conscious choice. If you are ignoring certain facets of a choice, assume that you are judging them.

DEALING WITH DEATH

The idea of conscious choices brings me back to death. Many churches, and society as a whole, look down on people who kill themselves, or who want to put an end to their lives medically. That makes no sense, given that we all choose to die.

> The one great difference between the person who chooses to die abruptly, as opposed to the one who chooses to die and then allows his body to take care of the process, is that the one who chooses to die immediately has no chance to change his mind. Many people do so.
>
> I would go further, to say that you cycle in and out of your fear of life and death regularly. Life can be frightening. In some instances, such as after the death of a loved one, in which you face the physical and psychological aspects of that transition—in your case, the medical and funeral bills, as well as your decision to walk a different path—would not dying be easier, far less fearsome, than living? And even without this type of major change, how often have you been afraid to face all or part of a day?
>
> Most commonly, people seek to hide from death. They may concentrate on the negative sides of the fear pairs—powerlessness, failure, lack,

aging, and sickness—as a way to avoid thinking about death; or they may concentrate on negative fear behaviors, such as unhappiness with their present lives, anger at others, or a sense of victimization. We will discuss the fear behaviors at length shortly.

People also may decide to spend all their time pursuing the world's gifts of money, fame, and power to try to escape death.

I find it hard to see that we chase after the world's gifts because we are afraid of death. People want better lives.

I trust that you like the theater. Allow me to illustrate this truth with a melodrama, which takes place at Egypt's Great Pyramid, guarded by the Sphinx. The curtain opens in a driving rain. A costumed clown with a bulbous nose, red lips, and a curly mop of blue hair enters stage left, wearing a yellow rain slicker. On his index finger, he twirls a large gold key. On stage right, a middle-aged woman in a black raincoat and hat picks her way along a mist-shrouded pathway.

As the two figures approach one another, a bolt of lightning illuminates them. Words boom through and around a clap of thunder: "Bring Death into the pyramid." At that instant, a lightning flash directs them to a sprawled, motionless figure, cloaked in a black cape and hood.

They lift him, cover him with the clown's jacket, and carry him to the entrance to the pyramid. As the clown inserts the key into the huge door, it glides aside to reveal a cavernous hallway. They enter, and place Death on the floor.

The clown lifts his slicker from the shrouded figure, and then points to the door. If they remove the key as they leave, the exit will be sealed. In effect, they can save humanity from the ravages of the Specter. The clown nods to the woman; it is her decision.

She bends down and pushes back the black hood. Inside is a skeleton, which immediately powders to dust. Then she shakes her head and smiles. Sealing the tomb would do no good. She recognizes Death as a symbol of a reality, a change that all of humanity must make.

The clown now points to a pile of gold artifacts and directs the woman to gather all that she desires. Again, she shakes her head. She recognizes that her victory over Death—unmasking him for what he is: literally, nothing—is treasure much more worthy of the name.

The woman walks out of the vast corridor in joy and freedom of spirit. Her black coat, hat, and hair shine lighter and brighter, until finally they become golden in the light of the Sun as the rainstorm passes.

Do you see the point of the story? The woman did not need the gold once she unmasked the Specter, because she no longer felt the need to hide from his presence. Understand that your search for, and your accumulation of, society's gifts ultimately stems from your fear of death. They become your protection, your imagined wall against this ultimate reality.

We all want to be remembered, to feel that our lives made sense. Many people look to money, power, or fame to accomplish that.

Only when you rely on what is inside you, not what is outside—and all outside you is change—do you develop a true sense of accomplishment. Only then do you accept the world as it is. Most importantly, only then do you accept yourself. Acceptance is the key to happiness.

UNDERSTANDING LIFE FORCE HELPS TO EASE THE FEAR OF DEATH

Change is one thing, but death requires another level of acceptance. My whole life portrait is gone in an instant when I die.

It is true that this life portrait is gone, but do not forget that there are many other lives that you can choose in the astral realm. Death is nothing more than sleep, with the exception that you feel life force leave your body. We will discuss life force before we look at the process of death, so you can understand this progression as the natural one that it is.

Life force is the energy that permeates all life. Air is not only air, just as water and soil, as well as plants, animals, and minerals, are more than they appear to be.

The space between the molecules of each is not space *per se*, but energy. The molecules that comprise each expression of life, and the atoms and subatomic particles in these molecules, whirl in this field of energy; it is what powers them. The so-called dark matter of the universe is also composed of such energy; in fact, you can think of the planets and suns as vast molecules whirling in a field of energy.

The dark matter that comprises outer space is the least compressed; there are expansive areas of energy between molecules. Air is next in density, water is intermediate, and minerals, including soil, are densest. Animal and plant life, including humans, is intermediate, in that all are primarily water-based.

It is important to recognize that everything, from the smallest algae to the planet itself, is powered by life force.

Scientists are beginning to see God behind the Big Bang, which is the starting place for all form and all energy that we term life force. The molecules that make up your body are the stuff of ancient suns and planets.

How does life force power the body?

The nervous system is the center of this great flow. It collects the life force energy between molecules of air, water, and food that you ingest and carries this energy to the spine, enlivening seven centers, called chakras, which in turn radiate it to all parts of the body.

Can I heighten this flow of energy?

Yes. Bless the food that you eat, the water you drink and bathe in, and the air that you breathe. If you recognize that all is alive, that God permeates the form as well as the energy that powers everything, you open yourself to this flow. You cannot see behind a closed door in physical reality, and a closed door in your mind acts the same way.

Once you realize that your energy is amplified in subtle ways—you are not as tired as you used to be, or you are overflowing with good ideas—you then begin to call on your mind to direct and increase this flow.

What happens when I am fearful? Does fear negate life force?

Fear does not stop this great flow, but it does impede its movement to the chakras and throughout the body. It is the reason that you often feel depleted after you experience fear. It takes a while for the blockage to dissipate and the life force to flow freely again.

I assume that the statistic I was quoted earlier—the seventy-five percent of time that we spend in fear—hardly enables most of us to amplify this energy flow.

That is correct. As people become less fearful, they find it increasingly easier to control the flow of life force. I cite two twentieth-century examples of people who utilized this control. President Kennedy slept little; he was able to amplify this energy, and it powered him. The swami Paramahansa Yogananda could say, "Energy is never tired," and sleep only three or four hours a day, because he too was able to heighten this flow at will.

Are you saying that they controlled their life force energy simply by being aware of it?

John Kennedy realized that he could call on his mind to direct and harness this energy without labeling it as such, and he spent enough of his time beyond the boundaries of judgment and fear to make it possible.

Paramahansa Yogananda operated from full awareness: he was cognizant of it, and controlled its flow. He also knew how to shut it off, and he died by conscious choice.

THE PROCESS OF DEATH

What happened when Yogananda shut off the life force? What does it feel like to die?

Death is not painful. It is much like going to sleep, with one exception: As death comes closer, you feel a surge of energy—the life force—ascend from your legs into your spine, and then into your neck and head. It exits through the third eye, which is the point between the eyebrows at which your binocular vision unites.

What about the visions that people see when they are dying?

They often see light that appears at the end of a tunnel. That is because the life force comes up through the spine into the neck and then into the head, and the spine can be considered a tunnel.

What are people really looking at, when they see this light?

They see the astral plane, their home between incarnations. Often, relatives and friends on the astral plane are present to greet the dying person.

Although we speak of this process in connection with death, you can also experience it in meditation or in concentrated prayer. Additionally, you can become aware of the life force, which also appears as a surge of light. You do this in sleep, but generally you do not remember what you experience.

Prayer and meditation differ from sleep in that you are aware enough to sense, or see, the life force and the astral light. The light of the astral dimension is most often seen as white, which contains all colors. The life force light can vary in color, from gold at the third eye to a symphony of colors lower in the spine, with the colors as individual as the person perceiving them.

What happens to the body when a person dies?

Life force that has not been expelled from the limbs and torso during the process of death stays there and, without the chakras to direct it, begins to break down the body. There are many factors that affect this process: the amount of air, water, or soil surrounding the body; the use of embalming fluids; and the like. The skeletal portions, which are more mineral-like, last much longer than the water-based parts, such as the lungs.

THE PROCESS OF BIRTH

To have a full picture of life and death, we next speak of death's complement, birth. The dynamo, the mind, enters the body at the instant of conception and directs the growth process, using life force from the mother. Fertility of the ovum and mobility of sperm are important factors, but the primary determiner of new life is the decision of a mind on the astral plane to choose particular parents. Without that decision, a woman does not conceive a child.

What about artificial insemination?

It is true in all variations of sexual union. In this instance, the mind chooses the primary parent and then waits for the chance to be born. This is also true if an individual is cloned.

Given that the mind enters the body at the instant of conception, the right-to-life people are correct; we should not kill a fetus.

I make no comments on the rightness or wrongness of abortion. Remember that bad and good, wrong and right are judgments, and, as such, they are entry points to fear.

If I were creating your system of law, I would eschew judgments in favor of a period of meditation or prayer for the mother-to-be, before she makes the decision to retain or terminate the fetus. Just as some children make the decision to die soon after they are born, others make the decision to die in the womb. There are as many variations of these decisions as there are individuals.

Does a fetus know if a mother will chose abortion?

A fetus does know if the mother will choose abortion—or, more accurately, since free will enters this equation, it has a strong foreknowledge that this will occur.

Is the same true of children that are born prematurely? Surely a child does not choose that scenario.

The child does not do so. Much of a mother's life force is directed to the fetus, which is forming an entire body system. When stress in any form is added to her depleted life force, the child can be expelled from the mother, as her body tries to regulate itself.

Once the baby is born, the life force energy from air, water, and food enters the body and the child begins to self-sustain.

Stress in any form should be avoided as much as possible before the age of eight. It interferes with the accelerated growth that occurs in those years, as the child learns to speak, eat, walk, and the like.

Of course, avoiding stress is good advice to people of all ages, because it depletes life force. If you feel tired or weak and cannot find a physical cause, assume that your life force is weakened by fear, with stress a major indication of underlying fear.

GOING PAST FEAR OF DEATH

We turn now to your fears of life and death. As with the other fear-pairs, when you fear one, you fear both. Although one primal fear is dominant, the subordinate fear is present.

163

First we consider death. Would you fully accept the fact of death if you could plan it completely? Would you accept it if you did not have to suffer physical incapacitation on this side of the curtain and if you had full knowledge of what is on the other side, including the assurance that you can indeed live again on this plane, as one of many choices that are open to you?

The only reason that you do not die this way is because you fear—and judge—death, rather than accepting it.

I cannot see how certain things—a drunk driver careening across the road, a child who wanders onto a highway and is killed, or a nuclear bomb that devastates the entire country—can be foreseen, or, in the case of the bomb, avoided.

As hard as it is to see from your society's perspective—you take the viewpoint of your society here—you can know all these things. That statement includes the presence of drunk drivers, bodily disorders, and threats, both nationwide and to your loved ones. Right now, you have the potential to be aware of all this, and more. You do so through life force control.

You do not keep life force. Once it is radiated into your body, it does its work of repair and renewal and then returns to the spine. From there, it is released via the lowest chakra. Every day, you pull in the life force of millions of people and other life forms through food, air, and water; and every day, millions of people and other life forms pull in your energy. This energy contains encoded thought-forms. Have you been depressed or distressed, yet did not know why?

Yes.

> The encoded thought-forms of others can do that to you. One fearful person can affect millions of life forms, from the plants that grow in sidewalk cracks to the heads of nations.
>
> I recommend a period of silence, along with meditation or concentrated prayer, at the beginning of the day, at midday, and in the evening. Not only does it help to cleanse the thought-forms of others that enter your body; it also helps to purify your thought-forms. In turn, your purified thoughts, radiating outward, help cleanse those of others.
>
> At the same time, ask to be aware of any issues that you may face. Your answers may come in the form of a dream, an intuitive guess, or a general awareness. You have had hunches, have you not?

One morning, I had the sense that I should be particularly alert for danger. That day, my car was almost broadsided by an out-of-control car.

> You can heighten that consciousness. Start each day by meditating or praying, and then ask for the blessings of God and your master-teacher. Following that, as you make plans for the day, ask for special awareness. As you make any major change, make the same request. Then listen for direction: from a dream, a hunch, a message from a friend, or some other way.

What if I find out something that I do not want to know? What if I have cancer?

> Most often, you will receive general messages indicating danger or change, rather than specifics. I give you an example: Every person in or near the World Trade Center and the Pentagon on September 11, 2001, knew intuitively that the airliners that crashed into those buildings were on their way. A few left the area, because they felt the oppressive weight of the emotional atmosphere. Most stayed. They ascribed their sense of unease to other sources, such as a longing to be with loved ones or apprehension about the upcoming workday. They believed that such an event was impossible.
>
> You know of a man who decided not to take one of the flights that later met disaster. All he could say was that he was running late, and he had a strong feeling that he should not even try to get to the airport on time. Similarly, most people who were not present for these tragedies did not have conscious awareness of what was happening, but they tapped their intuition to the point at which they decided to stay away.

By implication, then, even the authorities sensed the presence of danger.

> Even you sensed it, and you were twenty-five hundred miles from the scene of the disaster.

Could I—and everyone else—have known specifically that the World Trade Center and the Pentagon were the targets?

Yes. You could have honed and focused your feelings of distress to know the source of the threat, as well as its targets.

I mentioned that life force "messages" from millions of people flow through you. In this case, the people who emptied their minds of thoughts that would have taken them out of the present moment, and then allowed themselves to experience their feelings of restlessness and disquiet without labeling them, would have recognized how much terror they felt. If they additionally looked to the cause of their fear, they could have sensed the approaching airliners: as intuitive hunches, as words that they heard internally, or as visions of the upcoming tragedy.

So, in effect, we can all be psychics.

Yes, all people can develop their intuitive powers. Not all are called to be shamans or healers—in effect, to make psychic phenomena their full-time work—but each person can see beyond the ordinary objects and thoughts that fill her world.

Also understand that everyone has free will. A person who had a meeting scheduled for that morning at the Pentagon or the World Trade Center and was in touch with this "answering system" would have received a message indicating distress. The rest would have been an individual decision: to go to the meeting, or to cancel.

What I would impress on you is that you already know these things subconsciously; you simply bring them to your conscious mind through this technique. Your original question was: "What if I find out something that I do not want to know? What if I have cancer?" My answer is that you already know.

What if a person planned to die in those September 11 attacks as part of his pre-life blueprint?

The blueprint can be modified at any time. Everyone has free will, and can use it.

Remember that you speak from the perspective of one who wishes to live. At another time in your life, you may embrace a message indicating danger and the transition marked by death. We will discuss emotional residues—which can include these types of feelings—further when we consider ways that you can purge the core and primal fear-pairs (chapter 10).

GOING PAST FEAR OF LIFE MEANS GOING PAST FEAR OF CHANGE

Next, though, we must examine fear of life. Once you overcome your fear of death, you will triumph over your fear of life.

Again, I find it hard to understand why I would fear what seems like a good thing.

If you fear death, you fear life. Your fear of life may not be predominant, but it is present. Because the primal fears lie behind the core fears, assume that any time you enter the realm of fear, you are afraid of life as well as death.

In fact, I probably will surprise you when I tell you that most of humanity is more afraid of life than death, because life is defined by change. Acceptance of life means acceptance of change.

Fear of death has to be a whole order of magnitude greater than the fear of life.

You would put fear of death in the director's chair. No. Your fear of life is equally as strong as your fear of death; it is simply hiding. Any time you judge change, you pass judgment on your life.

Why would judging a change that is happening outside me as bad or wrong—or even right or good—equal a judgment of my whole life? Right now, our country is at war, and on a worldwide level, we are destroying the environment. I judge both as wrong.

You still equate acceptance of change with liking it. You do not have to do so. You accept that the war and the damage to the environment exist, and then do your part to re-create the world as you would see it. Acceptance does not preclude action; it simply excludes judgment—in this case, of politicians, business interests, and the like—and goes straight to the solution.

If you judge any change, you in effect judge yourself as severely as those whom you judge. In the face of the war and the damage to the environment, is it not infinitely more productive to stop wringing your hands and write letters to your federal and state senators and representatives, as well as support organizations that advance your views?

The fact is this: All of the fear-pairs have to do with change, and every time you judge change, you enter fear of life. Do you now see how pervasive this primal fear is?

You mentioned politicians. Many of us love to talk about politics. Are you saying that we should not do that?

If you are going to make judgments, you should not do so. That comment will ruin many good discussions!

I add that it is possible to discuss politics without making judgments, by talking about the general trends behind the politicians' actions and what you intend to do about them. Name-calling, the usual outcome of such discussions, is judgmental, and ultimately ends up as self-judgment.

Thus far, we have primarily talked about judgments of bad or wrong, because they are easy to grasp. The same is true of good or right, when they imply that bad or wrong exist.

I see no problems with judging myself as right or good!

If only life were that easy! You may consider yourself good or right today, but you invariably fear tomorrow's reverses. In the end, you have no peace until you accept the seemingly good and right, along with the seemingly bad and wrong, as things that exist, and then make your plans accordingly. If you are happy with a particular outcome, you may not feel the need to make any changes; that is the only difference. You accept all as facts, without labeling anything.

If I do not make judgments, will I no longer fear death?

> You will not fear death or life. Understand this: Each day that you are alive represents your choice for life.

Do you mean that I could be dead right now, if I chose death this morning?

> It might take more than one day to die, but the answer is yes.

I am not aware of making a choice for life each day.

> You usually make it in other contexts. For example, you felt sick this morning. Did you expect to die because of it?

No, I have a touch of the flu.

> Do I surprise you when I tell you that others in a similar situation have made the choice to die?

Why would they choose to die of a minor illness?

> They use it as a springboard to death, thinking something such as: *I am always sick, and I will never be well again.* You have heard those types of comments. Understand that the people who say such things could be making a choice for death. Others, such as the man who predicted he would die in his early fifties, have reasoned: *I am*

the age I specified for my death; it is time to die.
Both are choices.

I recommend that you make a conscious
choice for life each day, with a statement such as:
"I choose to live fully and happily today." I add
the word *happily*, because when you enter fear
through judgment, it becomes possible, even easy
in some cases, to choose death, your primal fear.
Given the prevalence of fear of life, do you see
the importance of that choice?

WHAT ARE YOUR ISSUES REGARDING LIFE AND DEATH?

You explored some of your attitudes
toward death when you examined aging and youth
(chapter 7). I urge you now to focus on your
primary fears about life and death.

Life

Are there situations or issues in your life
that make it acceptable to die, rather than live? If
so, what are they? Is it possible to change them, or
your ideas about them?

Death

What is most fearful about the process of
dying? What type of death would you prefer?

The Mini-Death of Change

Revisit the mini-death activated by
change. Overall, do you accept or judge change in

your personal life as well as in your community, state, and nation? What types of changes do you judge? Are there ways you can accept these changes?

Chapter Ten

STOPPING FEAR AT THE CORE AND PRIMAL FEARS

You can travel like the eagle,
from the lush, dark rainforest to
the open, dry plains, but if you
take your fixed ideas with you,
you have gone nowhere.

Guardian of Communication

There had to be a way to neutralize all this fear. The Guardian of Communication responded to my thoughts.

* * *

Yes, you can do so. This action, combined with the unraveling of the judgment behind your fear, will give you a happier, healthier, longer life. As Merlin, I was able to live to a great age because I walked beyond fear.

You help both yourself and the world when you halt the process of fear at the core and primal fear-pairs, rather than acting out your fear through fear behaviors. Fear behaviors are the primary sources of harm. You see them at their severest in the horrors of war, and in the unending search by humanity for power, fame, and wealth at the cost of other life, including the decimation and starvation of your own species.

NEUTRALIZING THE CORE AND PRIMAL FEAR-PAIRS

If you experience a core-fear pair, assume that you have made a judgment and that you have called up your fear of death and life. To unravel this mind-cocktail, you need to work backward. You must identify the fear-pair that you are confronting, face the judgment underneath your fear, and acknowledge your underlying fear of change—and ultimately of life and death.

Recognize the Physical and Mental Signs of Fear

The core fear-pairs bring up intensified sensations in your abdominal, midriff, or chest area. In other words, your judgment symptoms multiply. You may even feel pain in these areas. Many so-called digestive upsets, from burning in the esophagus to vomiting and diarrhea, as well as heart palpitations and chest pains, have their origin in the core and primal fear-pairs. Do see a doctor and take medication if necessary, but also reflect on their starting point: fear.

In whatever way they surface, assume that you have progressed from judgment to fear when the fear symptoms that you associate with judgment amplify to a point at which you cannot ignore them. Not only do they rule your body; they also direct your mind. Accept fear as your reality right now.

Unearth Your Core and Primal Fears

Identify the core fear that most affects you. Here are a few of an infinite number of examples: *I have another headache and I am afraid I may have a chronic illness; I feel powerless because my supervisor called me on the carpet yesterday for something that was really not my fault; or I believe that my strength is dependent on regular exercise, and now I cannot get outdoors to run.*

As you uncover one level of fear, you often find other levels below it. Examples are: *If I have a chronic illness, I will not be able to support my family; if my supervisor fires me, I may not be able to find another job; or if I cannot exercise, I will grow old and die.* There usually are a number of fear layers. Try to uncover at least two.

Identifying these layers of fear would make me feel more frightened.

You are already terrified. You are simply bringing fear out of the inner recesses of your mind. Once you accept all of your fear, you begin to disengage from it. If you do not take this step, you will begin to act out fear behaviors.

Now, recognize that the opposite side of the fear-pair is part of your worldview. If you fear poverty brought on by chronic illness, what do you fear about abundance and health? If you fear failure regarding the loss of your job, what do you fear about keeping your current position or finding something better? If you fear the effects of lack of exercise on the aging process, what do you fear about youth?

Finally, acknowledge that you fear death and life. Ask yourself questions about your fears. Does poverty lead to death? Does abundance mean death of a type, in that you may have to leave your friends and your way of life? Does failure ultimately make you want to die? Does success mean your life will become too complicated? Does aging automatically mean death? What about life as an elderly person scares you?

Uncover and Dismantle the Judgments Under Your Fears

Accept the fact that you have made a judgment about change, and that you deem the judgment as justified. What situation or issue brought up your judgment, and whom do you blame? Then dismantle the judgment as you did before, by recognizing that the person whom you judge is another human with the same types of hopes and fears that you have, and by accepting the fact that if you were not attuned to her, you would not be acting as judge and jury.

Decide What You Can Do to Reduce Your Level of Fear

Fear can be your teacher. For example, if you fear poverty, you may decide to join a savings or investment plan. If you fear abundance, you may decide to read about people who have become millionaires. Also, examine how your past affects the present. If your life portrait contains some old memories and beliefs that are counter to what you desire, revisit them in silence and revise them.

Finally, consider giving time and energy to societal and community causes, to modify the fears of powerlessness and strength that so pervade your society. What can you do to help?

Above all, remember to choose life each day, with a statement such as: "I choose to live fully and happily today."

CLEARING EMOTIONAL RESIDUES

It is time to address that last ten percent of fear, emotional residues from others and from your environment. Positive emotions—all aspects of love—and negative emotions—all aspects of fear—permeate not only the room you are in, but also expand to fill your home, your neighborhood, and, to a lesser but still discernable degree, the world. Emotions are immensely powerful.

A primary emotion can pervade a house, even after the homeowner leaves it permanently. A residue is left, comparable to the sound that circles outward after a bell sounds.

Are they related to the thought-forms that we discussed (chapter 9)?

No. Although thoughts and emotions are intimately related, emotional residues can exist independently of thoughts, which change rapidly. Think of them as the subconscious residue of conscious thought-forms.

How long does an emotion last?

It depends. Each emotion has at least two participants, an initiator and a receiver, with receivers acting as initiators and vice versa. Until they break their tie, surges of emotional energy persist. Once the initiator/receiver tie is broken, the emotion can fade within a day.

If I were to move into a home that was occupied by a person who did not break this tie, would the emotional residue stay there?

It would remain for a while, then fade away as the person redirects the emotional tie in his new environment.

I add that this type of emotional imprinting can exist in any relationship, even one separated by death, if the principals remain tied. It is unfortunate for both, because they are bound in a connection that lives only in the past. Both the person who has died and the person who lives are not able to go forward.

How do we avoid this emotional imprinting?

I recommend that you do two things each day, in addition to any clearing of the core and primal fear-pairs that is necessary.

The first step is acceptance. Remember that as long as you are not tied by judgment, emotional imprinting does not take place.

The second is a source of powerful benefits for yourself as well as the other: the blessing. As you bless the other, know that you are purifying your fear and judgment.

SECTION IV
FEAR BEHAVIORS--AND ALTERNATIVES

Just one shift in thought, from fear to love,
can accomplish miracles.

Guardian of Communication

Chapter Eleven

ANGER AND DEPRESSION

Assume that when you are angry,
you fear change.

Guardian of Water Clarification

Judgments and the fear-pairs primarily affect you. When you begin to act out fear through the fear behavior-pairs, the pain that you inflict on yourself and others, added to the fear-generated pain of most of humanity, ultimately stresses the planet.

The guardian began this series of communications on the fear behavior-pair of anger and depression when I commented: "I may be fearful, but I am not often angry."

* * *

Of all the people who live in fear—and that includes most of humanity—fully three-quarters act out the fear behavior-pair of anger and depression every day. You literally live in an atmosphere of anger. It is as natural to you as the air you breathe.

In fact, assume that more than a third of the time that you spend in fear is devoted to anger, and its shadow, depression, which is anger turned inward on yourself. You spend another third trying to control your world, or acting like its victim. The remaining fear behavior-pairs—staying busy to the point of exhaustion, and then feeling depleted; and retreating to the past or the future—fill the last third.

I define *anger* as rage that you direct at another and at yourself for bringing change into your life. Remember that there is always a person whom you blame—including yourself—behind any issue or situation that precipitates change.

You call anger rage, but there are many degrees of anger, from irritation to fury.

I define it as rage, because it is an extreme emotion, divorced from rational thought. Anger, even what you term annoyance or irritation, is never trivial. When you are angry, it fills your life. You may go to work, take care of your family, even play. You may appear to be a good mother, father, friend, employer, worker, son, or daughter. However, nothing besides your anger registers with any degree of importance, even major life changes such as birth or death. If you find yourself distracted or forgetful, ask to see the source of your anger.

Additionally, this expression of rage is always directed to yourself as well as another. If you are depressed—which we define as anger turned inward—ask yourself who else you detest. Conversely, if you are angry with another, assume that you are upset with yourself. In terms of priority, you are primarily angry with yourself, and only secondarily angry with another.

These two facets of anger—self and other—are always there, and a person is always the target, even if you think you are angry about a situation or issue.

THE GIFTS OF ANGER AND DEPRESSION

What are the benefits of being angry and depressed?

Anger confers many gifts. When you are angry or depressed, you walk in tandem with most of humanity. Does it feel odd to create an inner atmosphere of joy by smiling, as the Guardian of Communication recommended (chapter 2)? If so, recognize this subconscious bond as the cause. At the same time, you have a sense of freedom in your feeling of separation from your brothers and sisters. Anger is an expression of fear, and fear isolates you not only from the rest of humanity, but also from all expressions of life, up to and including God.

In addition, anger that you direct at another gives you the illusion of controlling change. Why else would adults hold onto childhood rage at a deceased parent, or direct their fury to a divorced partner, rather than confronting and resolving this fear behavior-pair? When you cling to anger, you lock yourself into a past mindset, and you feel justified in doing so.

Anger's greatest gifts, however, are your feelings of peace and power. Wrath overwhelms the core and primal fear-pairs. You do not worry about success and failure, lack and abundance, sickness and health, aging and youth, even life and death, when you have a cause and an opponent. On the contrary, you feel alive and resilient. You know people whose rage seems to spark them to life, and indeed that is what happens. Of course, none of this is true, because the chemicals associated with fear ultimately destroy your body and mind.

Anger that is primarily turned inward as depression has its rewards too. If you choose to be passive, you can revel in the sense of victimization, the shadow side of control. If you choose an active response, you can channel your depression into a whirlwind of activity, which allows you to forget the core and primal fear-pairs, just as anger does. Both approaches earn you the attention and support of others, either in the form of pity for your martyr-like state as a sufferer, or in the form of applause for what is again a martyr-like state, when you are too busy.

It seems to me that activity would be the ideal antidote for depression.

It is, but only when it is directed to resolving its cause. Unless you accept the fact that you are angry with yourself as well as another, and find the source of this anger, you simply layer another fear behavior on it. In the long term, that never works.

ALL ANGER HAS ITS ROOTS IN FEAR

Describe the process of getting angry. It seems as if one minute I am not angry, and the next minute there it is, full-blown.

Anger begins as a quiet murmur, after you have judged a situation or issue—and a person—as wrong or right, bad or good. At this

186

point, you are not angry; you are uneasy. You then enter one of the core fear-pairs: powerlessness and strength, sickness and health, aging and youth, lack and abundance, or failure and success, plus the primal fear-pair of death and life. It is at this point that anger appears. All these processes happen within seconds.

The important thing to remember is that your reaction is rooted in fear of change. It follows inevitably, as night does day. You may fear that you are as wrong or bad as another person's words or actions indicate; you may want to run away from a life-altering event, such as sickness, old age, or death; you may wish to escape confining circumstances in your present life; or you may lash out at others because your job, marriage, or home—and ultimately your self-portrait—seems threatened.

There has to be justifiable anger. Jesus threw the moneychangers out of the temple.

Until you are a master-teacher such as Jesus, assume that every time you become angry, you are fearful. Take for granted that there is no such thing as righteous anger, only craven fear.

ALL ANGER IS TWO-SIDED

I stress the fact that anger is always two-sided. We have discussed the fact that you are angry with yourself when you are angry with another. Additionally, at a subconscious level, you are aware of what we can term impersonal anger: the anger of one nation or race toward another, for example. There are no boundaries between your life and other life. Any barriers—body, place, and time—are, in truth, nonexistent.

I add that if anger were not two-sided, with one side acting as fuel for the other, it would die, just as a fire dies when its fuel is exhausted. That is true of both personal and impersonal anger. If you decide not to be angry with another, your anger toward self evaporates. If you decide to accept all races and nations equally, you are no longer aware of the impersonal anger that surrounds you.

What if I get angry with myself for something minor: breaking a dish or forgetting to return a book to the library? There is no one else to blame.

If you become angry with yourself for something that is inconsequential, assume that you have internalized childhood scoldings for being clumsy or forgetful. Generally, you have entered the core fear of powerlessness, based on these old memories. So, not only are you blaming yourself, but you are also dredging up childhood anger at a parent or other authority figure.

In these situations, recognize with a sense of compassion that the authority figure was probably acting out her fears, and allow yourself the freedom of being less than perfect on occasion. It marks you as an individual.

I repeat: You are never angry alone. In fact, assume that your rage goes far beyond the person who sparked it. Anger does not travel in a line toward a target; it radiates in a circle that can encompass multitudes. If you are angry with your boss, it is easy to find fault with your spouse, children, coworkers, friends, community, even your country. On the other side of the coin, without anger of your own, you can never be part of a circle of anger. It bypasses you.

It seems impossible to be calm in every situation. How about a husband who finds out that his wife is having an affair?

The situation exists, and it has to be dealt with, but anger is optional. I call on an extreme example. When Jesus was taken captive, he could have been enraged. He was not so; in fact, he freed his captors from the karmic results of their actions toward him when he said, "Father, forgive them, for they know not what they do." This act of acceptance and forgiveness, rather than judgment, liberated all those associated with his crucifixion from any need to experience one or many lifetimes to expiate their guilt.

In this case, if the husband accepts his wife's actions rather than judging them, he frees himself from the circle of anger. He and his wife still have to deal with the situation; they may decide to divorce. However, judgment, and the resulting fear and anger, do not have to play roles in the scenario. The real issue is whether they will remain together, not who is right and who is wrong.

I return to Jesus' life. In addition to the twelve who were his closest companions, thousands cherished him and his teachings. He was the subject of a citywide parade that Christians celebrate as Palm Sunday.

Many were enraged when he was captured; Peter's swordplay is only one illustration of their fury. If Jesus, as the central player, had harbored anger, your history books would describe a war that spread across the Middle East after his death. His serenity and peace influenced all who loved him, and forestalled the killing of untold numbers of people. *That* is the power of not taking on anger.

Is it possible for one person to avert a war now?

If you were a key player—a person around whom the drama of nations plays—yes, you could prevent a war by not harboring anger. Even as a non-pivotal player, by banding with others in your community, state, and nation, you can help stop war by protesting in a way that does not have anger at its base. Martin Luther King and Gandhi preached just such an approach. I use King as an example. Without his doctrine of nonviolence, you would have been caught up in a great deal more civil strife in the United States.

YOU BLAME THE PEOPLE BEHIND A SITUATION OR ISSUE—AND YOU BLAME YOURSELF

What about the worldwide environmental damage that is taking place? I would not know who to blame.

You are *never* angry only about issues or situations. You direct your rage at the people whom you see as key players—for example, the president of the United States or the CEO of a large oil company—and at yourself.

I can see why I might direct my anger at a public person, but why would I be angry with myself?

When you judge an issue such as environmental damage, and the people behind it, as bad or wrong, your core fear is generally powerlessness in the face of an overwhelming display of power. Additionally, since fear of strength always accompanies fear of powerlessness, assume that you are angry with yourself for not doing something constructive.

This brings us back to acceptance. If you accept the situations or issues as they exist, if you simply look at them as the results of ways of thinking that pervade humanity, you can direct your energy to playing a role, large or small, in resolving them, rather than wasting it in anger.

In a larger context, it is essential that you look at anger in a new light. A charging bear is not angry as we define the emotion. Most often, her charge represents a demand that you stay away from an area that she has chosen for her cubs' safety. If you walk through the same territory when they are grown, it is again shared land. Similarly, much of what you perceive as anger in many species, including your own, is simply a demand for territorial awareness, not a call to conflict.

Both talking and listening are essential. It is where territories overlap that conflicts begin, be they physical or founded on ideas. You are not so far removed from your relatives in the animal kingdom.

How do we defend ourselves without anger?

> I said that the bear does not feel anger, and no one would accuse her of being a wimp! You bypass anger by finding your core truth. In the case of the unfaithful spouse, it may be a need for honor and truth in the relationship. That is the husband's bottom line, the territory that he claims, just as the bear claims her physical territory.
>
> It is your job to make your core truth known to others, even if it touches the kinds of fears that we have discussed: the life-altering change that you do not want to face, or the threat to the portrait that you have created of yourself. After that, you have to be willing to take the consequences. It is the only way you can feel a real sense of freedom. Like the bear, you do not feel anger; you are simply defending your territory, and you deal with situations as they arise.

DEALING WITH ANOTHER'S ANGER

How do I deal with people who are angry with me, without taking on anger?

> First, recognize that the other person is afraid of something. You do not need to know what type of fear underlies his anger; simply be aware that judgment and fear are present.
>
> Second, understand with compassion that the other feels a momentary lightening of her load of fear by shifting the self-anger that she feels to you. She is not wrong if you are wrong; she is not powerless if you are powerless. The list goes on.

Finally, decide whether you wish to carry the burden of the other's anger. Be advised that it never helps to do so. What is your core truth? If you are living blamelessly in relation to the other person, there is no need for you to change any part of your relationship. In addition, know that you can never cure the fear that underlies the rage of others; that is their burden. Your concern is to grow in love. In other words, accept and forgive, as Christ did.

RELEASING YOUR ANGER AND DEPRESSION

Do I get past my feelings of depression and anger in the same way?

The only way to neutralize anger—at yourself and another; remember that the two go hand-in-hand—is to accept that you are angry, and then find the fear and judgment at its base. It is that simple and that complex. Find a quiet spot, calm your mind, and examine your thoughts. In both cases, your key lies in the fact that you have judged yourself, and another, in relation to change.

What Change Underlies Your Anger?

Your first step is to identify the change that triggers your anger. How does it affect your core beliefs? Do you feel helpless to alter it? What effect do you foresee, or have you experienced? What judgment have you made, and what is your major fear-pair?

Once you find what you are afraid of, accept your fear and deal with it as you would any other issue. If necessary, talk it over with someone who can give you an impartial view.

Whom Do You Blame?

Your second step is to identify the person whom you blame, and why you blame him. We have discussed the fact that you are always angry with another person, but, in turn, he may stir up anger from your past. Rage directed at a parent for childhood hurts, or at a spouse who left you, may color all of your relationships with others.

Accept and Release All

Now say, "Father, forgive us, for we know not what we do." Your goal is to accept and release the people who triggered your anger, and ultimately to forgive yourself.

Say this repeatedly—every day for a week, a month, a year, if necessary—until you actually feel a sense of acceptance. Remember that as you accept and forgive others, you accept and forgive yourself, because the great circle of anger always includes you.

Life is quite straightforward. All sustenance is inside you. You go past your anger, and the anger of others, by recognizing that fear hides behind it. Once you have found the fear, acknowledge it. Only then can you let it go.

WHAT ARE YOUR ISSUES PERTAINING TO ANGER AND DEPRESSION?

We have touched on the fact that in each life there are old hurts that trigger anger responses. I ask you to look at them in depth.

How Does the Past Affect the Present in Your Personal Life?

Think of two people at work or at home who trigger your anger, and try to find its roots in your past. For example, if you were criticized constantly as a child, does even the mildest expression of disapproval in the present frustrate and anger you?

What do these people bring up that makes you angry with yourself? Who do you blame for instilling these ideas?

Can you accept and forgive everyone in this circle of anger including yourself? Are there any other steps you can take to nullify it?

What Makes You Angry in Your Community, State, or Nation?

Now identify two situations or issues in your community, state, or nation that trigger anger. What change, or potential change, is behind your distress? How does this change affect your core beliefs, many of which have their genesis in your childhood? Since you always blame others along with yourself, identify and then release all. Your goal is forgiveness.

The object of all this introspection is to find your sources of anger. By holding them up to the light of understanding, you begin to heal your fear—and your life.

Chapter Twelve

CONTROLLER AND VICTIM-CONTROLLER

> You have formidable power,
> both for good and for ill. You
> can opt for love and its progeny,
> union and peace; or you can
> choose fear and its offspring,
> separateness and pain.
>
> Guardian of Communication

What would it be like to live in love? The Guardian of Communication addressed my thoughts.

* * *

So, you opt to live in the union and peace that characterize love.

Yes, I do.

It is time, then, to discuss control and victimization. Once you go past anger and depression, plus this fear-behavior pair, your life will be markedly happier.

To begin, do you hold the same ideas as other members of your birth family?

No. Some of our beliefs are very divergent.

Consider your situation a microcosm of the world, in which each person stands at a particular point on the great wheel of duality regarding political, social, cultural, and personal preferences. Even the most seemingly concrete areas of thought, the sciences, are hotbeds of dissension when a new idea is proposed. These differences in ideas reflect a physical truth: All is movement from birth to death, from the seemingly eternal universe to you personally.

Given that all is change, are you really surprised when, on a societal level, an Alexander or Napoleon appears, to try to bring unity and sameness to this flow? Are you surprised when, on an individual level, people cling to a set of ideas and ways of living that allow no discussion? There are many more idea-despots, or controllers, than people who live in flow. It is the way they make sense of their world.

The Guardian of Water Clarification said that we spend close to one-third of our time in an attempt to control others. That is hard to believe.

Control is your attempt to halt change, particularly change that affects your life portrait. You exercise control in one of two ways: as an active controller or as a victim-controller. The active controller commands the lives of others directly; the victim-controller does the same indirectly, by acting like a casualty of another's fear-related behaviors.

Just as the shadow that accompanies anger at others is anger directed to self, the shadow side of the controller—the emotion that accompanies this role—is the sense that others are seeking power over her. The controller also believes that she is a victim.

You say that control is an attempt to halt change, but what about change that is essential and good? People move, get married, change jobs, have children.

The changes that you describe may appear to be good. However, any change can be fearful, and ultimately judged as bad by the people involved, unless they are willing to change their thinking. Changing their minds transforms their lives; it does not work the other way around.

THE GIFTS OF THE ACTIVE CONTROLLER AND THE VICTIM-CONTROLLER

Still, why would people want to avoid changing their minds, if doing so would improve their lives?

In addition to fear's gifts—the sense of being alive and vital, of walking in step with your brothers and sisters, yet experiencing a sense of freedom in the belief that you are separate—you believe that by maintaining the status quo, ultimately you will not die. If anger makes you feel alive and vital, control makes you feel safe.

Think about it. You have created a life portrait, a way of living. If you change it, what will happen? You might be forced to confront all of your core fears: powerlessness and strength,

199

failure and success, lack and abundance, aging and youth, and sickness and health.

In the face of those potential threats to your mental and emotional stability, your fear of life and death also goes into overdrive. Not only is it possible that you will live in a state worse than the one you are leaving; you might die as you cross the abyss created by change.

This need to feel safe also fuels humanity's search for the world's gifts of power, fame, and wealth. People see control—of people and ideas, as well as business and political organizations—as the way to safety.

Their dream is that if they can gather enough of these ephemeral treasures around them, they can live as potentates, shielded from the cares and concerns of the world. However, how much is enough? Since these treasures are fleeting, even the richest people seek fulfillment in *more*. And, given that control is a fear-based behavior, it follows that there never is enough. No one can find peace when his search is fueled by fear.

THE DECISION THAT LIES BEHIND CONTROL

The purpose of control is to force others to live as the controller—or the controller who acts as a victim—wants them to live. In effect, the controller wants another to fill in the perceived weaknesses in his life portrait. To take a fairly benign situation, if the controller dislikes crowds, then the one controlled must compensate for that deficiency, even if it does not mesh with her life portrait.

There is magical thinking going on here, with the term *magical thinking* defined as the belief that another will develop the skills, inclinations, and interests that the controller deems important.

In truth, any time you want to direct another's life, you engage in magical thinking. Only when you see another person entirely do you even begin to discern his life portrait. This happens in an atmosphere of acceptance, the antithesis of the fear that the controller harbors.

You may say, "That does not describe me," and discard the whole notion. However, control is subtle and far-reaching. Many more people live in control than acceptance, which welcomes differences in ways of living and belief.

Do you spend time thinking about what you owe others or what others owe you? I do not use the word *owe* only in relation to money, but also to less obvious interactions. Do you find yourself judging people because they do not come up to your standards regarding how they direct their time or their energy, particularly as they relate to you?

Sometimes. However, I think of these types of thoughts as ways of balancing relationships, not as control issues.

Do you feel the same way when others voice the same types of views regarding you?

Not always . . . . You are implying that I am using a double standard.

Change one letter of the word *owe* to *own*, and you are much closer to the truth of these types of exchanges. Others try to own—or control—you, and you try to own—or control—others. The word *own* describes the decision of the controller: *My way is the only right way.* Judgments can apply to cultural preferences such as music and art, societal choices such as political affiliations, and personal preferences in friends, partners, cooking, religion, housing, and the like.

To determine if you are using a double standard, see if there is a judgment underlying a particular interaction. If a judgment is present, assume that the controller fears that another person will damage his life portrait.

For example, if you see yourself as a person who gives, and someone calls you a skinflint, you can either shrug off the remark or you can judge her as wrong. Underneath your judgment is the fear: *What if this person is right? Does her comment make my entire life portrait suspect?* Thus, the desire to own another. It represents safety.

Getting even, a form of self-protection, is the mark of both the active controller and the victim-controller. It often takes the form of withholding: of thanks, praise, or money, anything that could help another go forward in life.

Many controllers use the carrot-and-stick approach to withholding. For example, a supervisor may praise you just enough to keep you hooked into his agenda, but then set impossibly high standards for your next project. Parents may say that a son or daughter is free to choose any career, but then withhold promised college funds when that career does not match their expectations.

The goal of control is power, or ownership. If you are dealing with a controller, I advise you to beware of all gifts. They invariably have strings attached to them.

THE CONTROLLER WHO POSES AS VICTIM

For every pocket-Napoleon, there is the controller who poses as victim: imposing his way on others by indirection. This scenario often develops when controllers feel thwarted. Their goal is still ownership; they simply go underground with it.

For example, you know of a mother who believes that her adult children owe her physical and emotional support as repayment for her role. Now, sons and daughters often do provide that type of support to an aging parent, but the idea-despot raises the stakes by not only demanding this assistance but also by ignoring and demeaning their life purposes, if they do not harmonize with the role that she sees them playing. If—or when—they ultimately reject these demands, the controller seeks to undermine them, often through emotionally-charged issues such as sickness, with the sense of victimization: *Look what you have done to me by not acceding to my demands.*

Note that the goals and techniques of the victim-controller are the same as those of the active controller: requiring that others live according to his values, and withholding

203

emotional and/or physical support, either completely or in the form of carrot-and-stick actions.

If you are the object of an active controller or a victim-controller, know that you can never satisfy him; there will always be a higher stake, another demand for assistance. In addition, just as it is easy to expand your anger once you are angry, it is also easy to expand your circle of control once you become an active controller or a victim-controller.

But sometimes there really are victims—those family members whom the mother is trying to control, for example.

There may be other angry or controlling people, but there are no victims. Whether her family members turn away from her in disgust, saying that they have their own lives to lead, or whether they unwillingly comply with her every wish, they have entered the realm of fear.

In the second instance, perhaps they are being kind.

Not if they have made a judgment of bad or good, wrong or right regarding the mother, and are acting out of a sense of what the mother owes them for acquiescing. Given that the active controller and the victim-controller withhold from the other, the result is not compatibility or joy, but increasing frustration on both sides.

Sometimes it is easier to go along with what others want, rather than fight all the time.

It is easy to fall into this role; and, indeed, it is a comfortable place, because society often interprets *victim-controller* as *martyr*. Trust me, the real martyrs were free people who chose service to others and to God, not self.

Remember that the minute you try to own another, you also feel that someone is trying to own you. Even if you picture yourself as a victim of control, you are still trying to control, or own, another. If you did not judge the other, you would be immune to any attempts to own you. Do you understand the synergy?

I give you an all-too-common judgment: *I would be happy, if only this person would get out of my life.* In this instance, you have judged the other as bad. However, you also think of yourself as bad, because you have adopted the role as victim, rather than standing up to him.

Once you heap this judgment on yourself as well as the other, you end up fearful, with fear of powerlessness predominant. To get back a sense of control, you may adopt the role of the victim-controller, by seeking solace and rectification of the situation from others.

Alternatively, you may direct your energies to one whom you believe you can control, such as a child or pet. Just the other day, you heard a neighbor remark to her dog: "If you do not behave correctly, I will not take you for a walk." Now, the dog may need training, but is her attitude going to rectify that need?

GOING PAST CONTROL

How do I get past another's attempts to control me?

Recognize that the controller seeks a sense of unity and permanence in life. At the same time, since the controller would change your life, you need to exercise your territorial rights, as you do when faced with another's anger.

Find your core truth, your bottom line. If the controller cannot accept it—and, as I said, often controllers take on the role of victims rather than give up their ideas—then do what you must to protect your goal of self-expression. Accept that the controller feels as he does, that there is nothing you can do to change his attitude, and make your plans accordingly.

Your options are to state your needs and trust that he will accept them, or to back off from the relationship wholly or partially. Never, for one moment, believe that the controller is right. He simply cannot see another way.

What if I am the controller or victim-controller? How do I change my way of relating to the world?

Whereas anger is often a reaction, control is, as you imply, a way of life.

You need to recognize one fact: As you attempt to hobble the free movement of others with control, you constrain your own progress. In day-to-day life, do you find some family members or friends distant? Do you find that you limit your own activities and thoughts? These are examples of withholding that circles back to you.

Often, the choice to control also brings on physical consequences, in the form of illness or injury. Ask yourself: *Is it worthwhile to cripple myself through control?* If your answer is yes, I suggest you find a good therapist! The controller seeks a sense of completeness through ownership of others' ideas and actions. Long term, the controller finds fragmentation, a life that is lonely and unfulfilled.

When you seek to control, or own, another person's behavior as an active controller or victim-controller, in effect, you seek to harness the clouds. Not only is control unwise, it is evanescent. I say that it is unwise, because you set into effect a chain of circumstances, and the outcome of those events is often unanticipated and unwelcome. You play the role of God without all the facts. I say that it is evanescent, because of the nature of life, which is flow and change.

QUESTION EVERY USE OF CONTROL ON A SOCIETAL LEVEL

It is important to speak about governmental control. In effect, society is an expansion and a reflection of individual control issues.

On the community, state, and national levels, question every action that has control as its end. In particular, question any action that has money as its primary or secondary objective.

I advise you, as individuals and as nations, always to seek the solution that lessens, rather than heightens, the element of control. The goal of control is stability, and since change is the baseline for all life, any attempt to control is predestined to fail eventually. Know in advance that there will be unforeseen reactions, and that the result is fleeting in relation to the age and promise of Earth.

We need to exercise control—which I define as standardization—to make our society and technology work.

Your society is increasingly top-heavy with control. You live, not by exercising control, but by understanding basic laws. As a society, which serves as an umbrella to protect its people, it is necessary to weigh each attempt to stabilize individual thought and action, because there is a point at which stability becomes totalitarianism. In technology, there is a point at which stability becomes destruction of the natural world.

The ideal society honors the freedom of its people, as well as the forms and motions of the natural world, and makes its laws accordingly.

WHAT ARE YOUR ISSUES PERTAINING TO CONTROL AND VICTIMIZATION?

It is time to look at your individual control issues.

Childhood Issues

What were your family dynamics as a child? Did you live with controllers or people who felt victimized? Do you see any echoes of their patterns of behavior in your present life?

Personal Issues

Now look at the people with whom you interact at work and at home. Are there people who demand too much of your time or energy? Do you believe that others owe you time, energy, or other considerations? What is your bottom line? Can you reach a point of agreement?

Societal Issues

Next, consider the types of pressures that you face in your community, state, and nation. Do you feel like a victim in the face of overpowering strength? Does any organization demand more of you than you can comfortably give?

Conversely, do you believe an organization is slighting you? For example, if you receive Social Security, disability payments, a pension, or unemployment insurance, do you believe that you deserve more? What is your bottom line? Are there steps you can take to rectify this situation?

You will find that the sense of freedom that underlies your exploration of these issues makes the pain of facing them worthwhile.

Chapter Thirteen

THE WHIRLWIND AND DEPLETION

In this society and this age, in
which the machine rules, many
people are more fearful of free
time than they are of work.

Guardian of Water Clarification

I had never thought about fearing my free time. I asked: "Are you saying that we live like machines?"

* * *

Yes. As a society, you are in love with your technological marvels. What you do not realize is that your minds, once they have chosen a focus, become one with it. In the case of machines, it is untiring, unceasing work. Given that focus, are you surprised that people work more hours per week and take fewer vacations than they did in the mid twentieth century? You have indeed become afraid of free time.

I label this machinelike state, in which you are immersed in activity most of the time, or else getting over the resulting tiredness from all this busyness, the whirlwind and depletion.

THE WHIRLWIND

First, we address the almost-constant state of activity that I term *the whirlwind*. The focus of this activity can be what you call important—family, work, community, state, national, or international interests—or it can be strictly personal enjoyment. Your society welcomes and rewards activity, so it is hard to see yourself as adrift when you enter the whirlwind, but it is indeed the case.

I call this state the whirlwind to differentiate it from activity that is required to procure the necessities of life: food, clothing, and shelter. The whirlwind goes beyond these essentials to fill every moment with distractions, followed by a sense of tiredness and depletion.

If sleep is your only silent time, be assured that you have adopted a machinelike focus, no matter now noble or moving your explanation for your life of action. And, since this is a fear behavior-pair, under that focus is fear, along with a judgment about change.

Underneath your constant activity, your mind is trying to soothe your fears the way it knows best. Its reasoning is thus: *If she buries her fear, she will feel better. What will calm her?* As a result, you decide to work too much, fill your days and nights with community service, or do any number of things that you deem useful or fun in order to fill your life.

You say that my mind is trying to soothe me. Is it trying to clear itself of fear?

You feel fear in all parts of your body, not only your mind. Even the tips of your toes and fingers respond to stress. When I say *you*, I refer to you in totality: Your mind is trying to clear your body, as well as your thoughts and emotional reactions.

I give you some examples of the whirlwind: *I am a scholar, and I have to read all the time to keep current in my field*; *I am an important member of state government, and I must forego any thoughts of a vacation, in order to make sure my office runs smoothly*; *my work for the homeless is all-consuming, and I am on call 24-7*; or *I need to shop every day, in order to care for my family.* All of these explanations sound like perfectly justifiable reasons for activity. Yet, I assure you that they can—and most often do—serve as shields for fear.

It probably is necessary for the people in these examples to do exactly what they are doing. Yet you say they are running away.

They are running from fear if they allow activity, not silence, to dictate their lives. I label activity a fear behavior when it is used cover up fear that stems from a judgment. The government official may dream of sailing around the world, yet go to the office every day to face hours of meetings and paperwork. The mother may picture herself as an entrepreneur, setting her own hours and doing work she loves, yet spend a full day taking care of her family.

There is some form of change—perhaps an unfulfilled dream, or the challenge of sickness—that these people are afraid to face.

They judge life-as-is as bad or wrong, but do not want to face the change that a decision may engender.

Whatever the cause, they accomplish nothing by living in the whirlwind. The irritant remains. The only real solution is to accept that a nagging fear of change exists, identify it, and then deal with it. Their resolution may be as basic as recognizing the need for silence or their own space, or as sizeable as bringing a dream to reality.

Sometimes it is next to impossible to change our lives, particularly when others are involved.

Once you identify the cause of your discomfort, you may not be ready to readjust your life immediately. I do say that it is essential to name it, if you would have any peace. Does it do any good to run away from it?

If I were that mother or government official, what good would it do to recognize that I would like to sail around the world or be a business owner? I would still have my current responsibilities, and I probably would be unhappier than I was before.

You are ignoring the power of mind, both when you immerse yourself in activity and when you say that you are happier not knowing the source of your uneasiness. In effect, you are running away from your one true strength, your will. You also are ignoring your gifts of time and energy.

The government official may be able to use his management expertise to devise a savings plan that will bring that dream trip to life, and the mother may have several hours for study while her children are in school. Similarly, if a person knows that her marriage is in jeopardy or a health problem must be resolved, is it not better to deal with the issue than to put if off?

Some things are fun to do. The mother may enjoy shopping. She may consider it a reward for taking care of her family.

The pervasive impetus to shop is a good discussion point. Many people buy things because they enjoy the activity of buying. Thus, shopping serves as a distraction, rather than filling a need. Merchandisers spend millions of dollars on ads that picture buying as wholesome and fun. You shop in a manmade environment, protected from the unknowns of weather, terrain, and wildlife that accompany being outdoors.

Additionally, bringing new things into your life, including those pervasive technological marvels, insulates you, at least temporarily. You feel fulfilled, and safe from harm, with possessions surrounding you.

Thus, you fill your days with activity that seems satisfying, but it is simply a diversion. Moreover, recognize that the mindset of buying for pleasure, rather than need, permeates and clutters your lives. It makes you dependent on money in increasing amounts. It makes money king, rather than servant. It is why you often consider how much money you earn more important than what you do.

Still, shopping is a way of unwinding for many people.

When you say *unwinding*, you are referring to two things: enjoyment and relaxation. Examine both. If shopping is fun, ask yourself what is not fun. If buying serves to relax you, determine what is causing your stress. Do you bury your judgments and fear in things?

The primary gift of buying more than you need is that it dulls your commitment to what lies in your core, the dreams that you would bring to life. Think about it: If you would be a sailor through the uncharted seas of your dreams, what more comfortable way is there to put them to sleep? You ensure that you will never have the time, energy, or money to face the change that living a dream can bring.

I recommend that you evaluate your desires. Do you really need—or even want—what you plan to buy? You must make the decision to acquire what you need, and very little of what you want, or you will be too bloated to walk your path to freedom.

THE OTHER SIDE OF THE WHIRLWIND: DEPLETION

The other side of the whirlwind is the feeling of depletion. Understand that the term *depletion* does not refer to tiredness *per se*; it is the feeling of not having achieved your goal. In that sense, it is the companion of depression, the shadow side of anger. Assume that you are depressed when you feel depleted.

You may have accomplished something that will place your name in your children's history books, but if you worked in a state of fear,

216

you have not succeeded, at least in your mind. That may sound strange, but whenever you make a judgment—for instance, *this is the crowning achievement of my life, and it has to be perfect*—you become fearful. In this case, you jump into the core fear-pair of failure and success, from there you enter the whirlwind, and finally you feel depleted.

No matter how perfect your achievement appears to others, in your eyes it will seem imperfect. Additionally, your feeling that it is not quite right may be true, because you can lose sight of your goal in the whirlwind.

Because people accomplish so much in a state of constant activity and fear, it is hard to see what they can achieve in a state of focused activity and peace. I turn to Frank Lloyd Wright, the famed architect, because he was able to center himself in joy, not fear, when he designed many of his buildings. Even today, his work dazzles the eyes.

I use the free-flowing spiral of the Guggenheim Museum as an example. Wright did not have more talent than other master architects; what he had instead was the freedom of vision that allowed him to go past the restrictions imposed by the beliefs prevalent in his time. If Wright had allowed judgment to enter his creative process, he would have designed a boxlike museum, much like those that are so common in your large cities. To go beyond the prevailing definition of how this type of structure should look, Wright operated from a place of acceptance—and self-acceptance, his own definition of beauty, was fundamental—rather than applying a judgment of bad or good, right or wrong to his work.

The moment you put a judgment in place, you stifle creativity. It is a short step from there to working too hard, to substituting long hours and concentrated, focused attention in place of inspiration. In this case, Wright could have reasoned: *This design varies too much from the norm; it will not be accepted. I must set this aside and create another.* Do you see the judgment of himself as wrong under that thought?

We have been discussing a work-related issue, but the same idea holds true for other ways of using the whirlwind. Even overemphasis on entertainment can fill your waking hours and leave no time for silence. Know that you are hiding from something, that there is a judgment lurking somewhere.

Depletion is in actuality a form of mourning. It can present itself as boredom, vague unease, weariness, apathy, or a sense of something incomplete. If you do not feel a sense of peace and completeness at the end of a busy day, a demanding project, or even a fun excursion, you may be dealing with depletion. Look underneath for the judgment.

Explain more about this type of weariness. After a long day outdoors I feel tired, but that is not what you are discussing.

The state that I allude to mingles mental and physical fatigue. If you climb a mountain, you may be exhausted, but you also feel a sense of contentment and completion.

What do we do when we find ourselves feeling depleted, because we have been in the whirlwind?

> As always, the key is acceptance. Accept what is, and go from there. Ask yourself: *What can I do from this point on? How do I choose to live?* If nothing can be done immediately, look at this time as a chance to grow.
>
> A full, open life, lived in acceptance, is far grander than the largest building. In effect, that openness is your ultimate construction, the reason you are alive.

GIFTS OF THE WHIRLWIND AND DEPLETION

If most of us live this way, we must do so for a reason. What are our gifts?

> Since the whirlwind and depletion leave you with little time or energy to deal with the issues of change, they offer you a sense of peace. What better way is there to feel satisfied than to fill your life with activity that feels worthwhile or is fun?
>
> Of course, because the whirlwind and depletion are fear-based behaviors, you never find the serenity you seek. Only when you eliminate the judgments of good and bad, right and wrong, that underlie your fear of change, can you truly feel peace in the midst of activity. At that point also, you engage in worthwhile activity. You are no longer running away.
>
> Additionally, the whirlwind and depletion offer a sense of kinship with the rest of humanity, most of whom are also too busy. Moreover, you

219

earn the kudos and sympathy of family, friends, and associates, both for working too hard and for feeling depleted—as long as you do not feel exhausted for too long. One of the givens is that you must race back into the whirlwind right away in order to maintain the appearance of being too busy, so you can legitimately feel depleted. It is an endless circle.

The whirlwind and depletion's greatest gift, though, is the sense of being able to hold onto life. You reason thusly: *If I am not busy, I am not alive.* Assume that your key fear is death.

You use any number of thought patterns to cover up this belief, primarily in the form of compulsions: *If I am not there all the time, the place will fall apart*; *if I do not keep up academically, others will replace me*; or *if I do not finish this today, it will never get done.* I call these compulsions, because these are wants, not needs. Your physical well-being is not dependent on them, but your mind feels secure with them.

THE IMPORTANCE OF SIMPLICITY AND SILENCE

How do we get past this reactive way of living?

You must make simplicity and silence the cornerstones of your life.

Live With More of What You Need and Less of What You Want

Take a hard look at your physical environment. Evaluate everything you have for its contribution, and give away or sell things that are no longer necessary. Try to do with less wherever possible.

Concentrate on things that help you achieve your life purposes, as well as the basics for physical and emotional comfort. You do not want an icebox instead of a refrigerator, or a quill pen in place of a computer—or at least I assume not. You also prefer to eat on porcelain dishes, you love books and music, and you want a sense of beauty and order in your home as well as in the clothes you wear.

Focus on what you consider essentials, emphasizing needs rather than wants, and you will never go wrong. You will also save money.

Make Active and Reflective Silence Part of Every Day

Most important, add at least a half-hour of silence to each day.

I recommend that you set aside a minimum of fifteen minutes for what I term *active silence*, a time when you withdraw from others and do something that you love. Your goal is breadth of spirit. Active silence can take many forms. For example, you may enjoy cooking, because preparing food gives you a chance to dream and plan, in addition to its sensory delights. Exercise and time spent in nature are two other excellent sources of expansion through action.

Second, reserve at least fifteen minutes for *reflective silence*. Again, this is time that you spend alone. Begin with a spirit-expanding text, from the Bible to poetry. Focus on the words. If thoughts come up regarding what you should or could be doing, set them aside and re-focus.

221

At first, the process of sitting in silence may seem impossible; in time, you will look forward to it. What you are doing is starting a meditation program. When you are ready to go past reading to this type of mind expansion, books on the subject will guide you.

Your goal is to widen your perspective beyond the movement and noise of everyday activity. Plan to use active and reflective silence throughout your life; they are as important for your physical and mental health as they are for the overall beauty that they bring to it.

I present some examples of the power of active and reflective silence. In addition to working as a physician in Africa, Albert Schweitzer was a musician, a husband and father, and author. Mahatma Gandhi led India to victory over the most powerful nation on Earth, and introduced the world to the power of nonviolent resistance. Eleanor Roosevelt not only served as First Lady; she also was a noted humanitarian who later became chairperson of the United Nations Commission on Human Rights. These were people of action—no one would deny that—but they based their action on the core of silence that we are discussing.

Without inner silence, you lead an ordinary life; you never go past your time and station. You are a forgotten writer and physician, not Schweitzer. You are an average politician, not Gandhi. You are a bureaucrat in a large organization, not Roosevelt. Moreover, keep in mind that without silence, with only a life of activity, you will find yourself lonely and afraid, with a sense of something not accomplished each day and throughout your life.

WHAT ARE YOUR ISSUES PERTAINING TO THE WHIRLWIND AND DEPLETION?

Explore your issues regarding these pervasive fear behavior patterns.

What Part Does Activity Play in Your Life?

Do you set aside time to enjoy leisure hours with family and friends regularly, or are you often too tired to do so?

Do you feel you have to fill most of your time with activity? If you must be busy all the time to feel good about yourself, do you carry a fear of failure, and a judgment of bad, if you do not do so? These judgments often are grounded in the family dynamics that you experienced in childhood.

What Is Your Relationship to Money?

Do you buy primarily to fill needs or wants? Are there things you can do to give yourself a sense of comfort, such as investments or increasing your savings?

Only when you see yourself clearly can you begin to make new choices.

CREATING BALANCE

For a week, I suggest the following: Each morning, list three major activities that you have

223

planned for the day. That evening, rate each activity as a need—an essential—or a want—something that was good to do, but was not crucial. Be ruthlessly honest.

At the end of the week, take stock. Are there places in which you can cut down on activities, or are you happy with your life as-is? In addition, did you include time for active and reflective silence each day? How did it feel?

Remember, the more you cram into your days, the odder cutting back on activities and adding time for silence will feel—at first. Keep it up. It will bring you to full enjoyment of life.

Chapter Fourteen

SANCTUARY IN THE PAST AND THE FUTURE

The future and the past are
stable, because they are your
productions. Unlike conventional
dramas, you do not have to deal
with temperamental stars,
producers, directors, or writers;
you play all the roles.

Guardian of Communication

The observation about the past and the future by the Guardian of Communication prompted my comment: "This is the first non-fear-related statement that I've heard in a long time." The reply set me straight.

* * *

Humanity's tendency to live in the past and the future is actually a major indicator of fear. If you spend several hours in timeframes other than the present each day, assume that you have chosen to live in this fear behavior-pair. In fact, you often combine both past and future in these retreats from the present; that is why I conjoin this search for sanctuary with the word *and*.

Are there differences between living in the past and living in the future?

No, in that they have the same driver: fear of change that is taking place in the present. Even if you consider the past and the future as places of great fear, they are more comfortable than the present, because they are your creations.

What about fear associated with impending change: for example, fear of losing a job because the company is rumored to be unstable; or fear of a natural disaster? I can imagine what I would feel if I lived on the Gulf Coast and knew a major hurricane was approaching.

We have discussed the fact that fear of change in the future is equally as strong as fear of change that is occurring now. I take the analogy one step further to say that there is no future; the only thing you "own" is this moment. Even if the change is six months away, if you fear it now, it is occurring now.

Moreover, if you make a fear real in your mind, if you are experiencing it in the mental realm, you can be the agent of its occurrence in the physical realm. In the examples that you mentioned, the large forces, such as company closings and hurricanes, are not necessarily brought into form by one person's thoughts, but if many people keep an idea alive, they can provide the mental climate for these changes to occur. The power of your minds is vast.

Sanctuary in the Past and the Future

Most of our fears never actually come to pass.

A side effect of fear is that it clouds your vision; thus, your thoughts become fragmented. If they were directed fully to that which you fear, you, along with others, could bring it into form.

On the other side of the coin, the past and the future can be fun. It is enjoyable to revisit delightful memories or dream of an alternative future. Are you saying we should never do that?

A retreat to the past or the future can be enjoyable, as long as you do not *live* there. The past contains the dreams and plans of childhood, unsullied by the reality of earning a living; and the future holds the dream of what you can be, also liberated from your day-to-day needs and wants. However, you cannot tarry there too long, or you begin to hide in your dream world.

On the one hand, you feel protected from the terrors of change. At the same time, though, you feel trapped, just as you would at a play that continues for days, rather than hours. At the subconscious level, you always know that the real business of life exists in the present.

Change is the most fearful aspect of life, and, of course, all is change. You are different today than you were yesterday, if only in the fact that you are one day closer to death. Each day, you readjust your priorities and make new decisions.

What about a bride who is planning a wedding? It will be necessary for her to live in the future as she makes arrangements for the church, the caterer, and the like. Or what about the family that is building a new home? They will spend many pleasant hours envisioning it, buying furnishings, and so forth. In addition, the bride and the homeowners will enjoy revisiting these special times afterwards.

The seemingly good experiences are hardest to sort, are they not? The bride may experience an instant of joy at the wedding ceremony, and the homeowners may be happy when they sign the final papers, but if they *live* in the future—if they spend more of their time there than they do in the present—fear plays the primary role as they experience change.

The bride may be concentrating on the externals of the wedding because she is afraid of the relationship. The homeowners may be afraid of the costs involved in building and the long-term stability of the neighborhood. In both cases, their joy is subsumed by judgments of bad or good, wrong or right, often in the form of regrets for the past or doubts regarding the future.

The key is this: Whenever you live in the past of the future, you are afraid of something in the present. Search your thoughts for your fear of change.

In these visits to the past and the future, is there a difference between a happy scenario and a fearful one?

Often they are mingled. Say you are a salesperson, and you have made a judgment of yourself as bad, because you have not met your quota. You are sure that your boss will fire you. Each day, you are happy to still have a job, but

228

you dread the moment when you will be called into your supervisor's office. You may retreat to a daydream of the past, in which you relive an award ceremony as top salesperson for another firm, or you may call up another situation in which you were summarily fired. Often you revisit both types of scenarios within the same daydream.

I illustrate these points with two tales.

TRAPPED IN THE PAST: THE KNIGHT'S STORY

First, the story of a knight who chose to become trapped in the past.

Thomas, a member of Arthur's Round Table, had an overriding goal: to steal the Holy Grail. Of course, Thomas did not use the word *steal*. He edified his desire by saying to himself: *I will kneel before Arthur, my King, with this Holy of Holies.*

Convinced that the Grail was in the British Isles, he dressed as a mendicant monk and wandered through the countryside. After four years, he felt more like a priest than a knight, but his vision of the Grail glowed as brightly as it did when he started his journey.

Finally, at an obscure church in Scotland, his quest was rewarded. As he knelt unseen in a darkened side chapel, he saw the parish priest withdraw a battered, nondescript silver cup from the sacristy on the main altar. Just seconds after the priest raised it above the head of a young girl with withered, useless arms, the youngster spread them wide and shouted with joy.

Thomas believed that the Grail would be as humble as Christ, and he was sure that this was the Holy of Holies that he sought.

Was it the real Grail?

The Grail is an idea rather than a reality, in that it connects people to their Christian roots. However, Thomas believed in the Grail as a physical object, as did most at the Round Table, including Arthur. My opposing view of the Grail—as a symbol of original Christianity rather than a physical object—was not popular.

In the presence of the miracle of healing that Thomas had just witnessed, he had second thoughts regarding the rightness of taking this treasure, no matter how worthy the cause. He decided to reveal his identity to the priest, and warned him that such a theft could take place.

The priest, in his fear, told the local sheriff, who then captured the knight. Thomas was a bargaining chip of the highest order, and Arthur made many concessions to secure him. No member of the Round Table, no matter how ignoble, would die in a common jail.

Within a month after Thomas returned in chains, Arthur sentenced him to death. I spoke with the king at length, but he held that he could not show mercy to the young man and still be perceived as an effective leader.

However, he was not without compassion. With his tacit agreement, I helped Thomas to escape and spirited him to my kin in Wales. A skilled surgeon changed his facial appearance to the point at which his mother would have trouble recognizing him, and then we asked him what he would be. With my uncle to accept him as a distant cousin and the community newly settled, he had an array of choices: farmer, sheriff, merchant, fisherman, and forester, to name a few.

Given these options, Thomas, in effect, elected to die. He could not see himself as anything but a member of Arthur's Round Table. He dreamed of a future in which Arthur would pardon him, and he relived his long search for the Grail.

He began to drink, and he lost the considerable sum provided to him through the king's generosity. My uncle gave him a small hut at the edge of the township, where he lived for his wineskin, his dreams, and his beggar's alms.

Of course, Arthur never pardoned him. It took Thomas a long time to die physically, after he died in spirit. In his old age, he began to question the townspeople regarding whether it was right to give up the Grail when it was within his reach. Essentially, he asked the blessing of his peers. People knew, of course, that a knight had escaped many years ago, but they did not believe that the old man had ever been strong enough in mind or body to be part of the Round Table.

Only one, a boy, listened to his stories. He served him like a son, bringing him light and nourishment. When Thomas died, he left the boy what little he had. He was transformed by love, and he died in peace.

The boy took the old knight's real gift, his tales, and traveled far, singing of the Grail that shone brightly on the altar, the miracle, the priest who betrayed Thomas, and the king who condemned him to die. Just as they had disbelieved the old man in life, people tolerated the songs of the young man as pleasant foolishness.

The truth is that Thomas had every opportunity to begin a new life, but he chose to hold onto the old. His life at the Round Table no longer existed. He could have recognized and accepted the qualities that he possessed—courage, honesty, and physical strength—and used those to help himself and others.

By continuing to live in the past, and dreaming of a future that would never exist, Thomas gave up present challenges and joys. The boy, on the other hand, took what was given to him and shaped a path from it.

No matter how painful it is to do, you must walk anew each day. Mind you, you do not need to gravitate to every new fad! Remain loyal to that which you love. Always recognize, though, that the world changes. Be aware of those changes, accept them, and make informed decisions regarding them.

TRAPPED IN THE FUTURE: THE MARINER'S STORY

Second, a tale of a mariner who chose to become trapped in the future.

Alfonse served as a deckhand on the *Santa Maria* on the voyage of a lifetime, traveling with Columbus to the New World. As a lifelong seafarer, he knew the world was round. Still, he carried a thought from childhood, instilled by the parish priest, of the Earth as a platter rotating in the sky.

Especially now, so far from home, he feared that the priest was right. Soon the ship would reach the edge of the dish of ocean, only to find a vast waterfall that would plunge it into the blackness of space.

Alfonse had two choices: to ignore the waterfall, or to concentrate on its presence just beyond the horizon. He opted to join the group of seamen who were sure they would die. Each morning, he anxiously scanned the sea for signs of mist that would indicate the cataract. In the still of the night watch, he cupped his ears, listening for the distant sound of water flowing into a vast abyss. In sleep, he alternated fear-filled dreams of drowning with visions of himself as a hero, kneeling before the queen in glory for having saved the ships by commandeering them and returning home.

He prayed, something he had not done for years. He also remembered his wife with longing, and he wondered about his six children, all of whom were born when he was away at sea. Would he ever see them again?

My point is this: Alphonse loved the sea, and this was his greatest voyage, but he did not experience it. He and his comrades never found the vast waterfall; however, that fact is immaterial. What is important is that he lived in that cataract, not on the ship.

Looked at from the perspective of the twenty-first century, you see his fears as groundless. However, trust me that you have your own version of the waterfall.

GIFTS OF LIVING IN THE PAST AND THE FUTURE

There have to be gifts for living this way.

The greatest gift of living in the past and the future is the belief that you can control, if not prevent, change. On one hand, similarly to a prisoner in a jail cell, you feel caught, unable to escape the fetters of your dreams. At the same time, you acknowledge that your cell is, if not comfortable, at least predictable.

In short, you trade freedom for security—only it is a security that, unlike the jail cell, is founded on nothing more than imagination. It is why the knight, and many modern counterparts, drink or take drugs. They numb you to the truth that you are living a life based in your mind, and your dream world can be shattered at any time.

LIVING IN THE PRESENT

As we have discussed, the antidote for your retreat to the past and the future is to live in the present.

What if you are in mental or physical pain? Isn't it better to retreat from the pain? Sometimes, the present is not comfortable or pleasant.

Acknowledge the pain, then travel inward and ask for healing in whatever way is best for you. You may wish to distract yourself by visits to the past and the future, but accept the pain, its presence in your life, first. Pain can be physical or mental, but it is always emotional. Ask what it can teach you, and listen in silence for its lessons.

Every morning, think about what you can accomplish today. Take steps to resolve an issue or a need, and you begin to mitigate the fear associated with the change that it brings into your life.

For example, you have a meeting scheduled for tomorrow. You have a number of choices. You can live in the past, either by regretting other meetings that have not gone well or by recounting your successes at similar sessions. You can live in the future, either by anxiously focusing on all the sandcastles that will crumble if the meeting is a disaster or by envisioning a major contract and a prosperous future. In both cases, you have judged the meeting in some way, as bad or good, wrong or right.

Your third alternative is to accept that this session with your client can result in a contract or a dismissal, prepare for the meeting to the best of your ability, and then let the situation play out as it will.

In the end, only what you do in the present—the preparations that you make—counts. The meeting will be successful or unsuccessful, based on what you do now. Do you see that you, in effect, give up, if you live in the past and the future? Your judgment may be: *I am sure I will fail*, or *I am sure I will succeed*. In neither case are you actually preparing for the meeting.

Do everything you can today, and every day, to complete your life. Live as if today matters, and let tomorrow take care of itself.

WHAT ARE YOUR TRIGGERS FOR RETREATS TO THE PAST AND THE FUTURE?

Now, take a look at your relationship with the past and the future. Believe me when I assure you that you will live more comfortably when you do so.

How Did Your Family Deal With the Past and the Future?

Look back at your childhood family dynamics. Did your parents, relatives, or guardians enjoy the present, or were they anxious about the future? Did they complain about misspent opportunities in the past?

Does your life contain any of those echoes?

What Types of Situations, People, or Issues Drive You to the Past and the Future?

For a week, look for specific triggers that bring you to the past or the future. What situations, issues, or people are involved? What types of scenarios do you construct, and how much of your time do you think about them? What fears and judgments lie under them?

Your goal is to live in the present, and that is possible only when you uncover these fears and judgments.

Chapter Fifteen

STOPPING FEAR AT THE FEAR BEHAVIORS

Inside the vortex of change lies
peace, the peace of the
hurricane's bright, clear eye.

Guardian of Communication

I began this discussion with the comment: "It is probably not even important to stop fear once I get to the fear behaviors, because by that time the damage is done."

* * *

Dismantling fear behavior-pairs is as essential as stopping fear at the point of judgment. Only by working backward from the behaviors to the core and primal fears, and from there to your judgments, do you begin to see patterns in the way that fear develops and progresses. You may not have stopped your fear before it became a behavior this time, but you are better prepared when it happens again.

I also remind you that you are not required to be perfect. Your only requirement is to grow into a wider expression of love.

GETTING TO THE HEART OF FEAR BEHAVIORS

Fear that has progressed to the level of behavior is the hardest to eradicate, because it can be insidious. Since fear behaviors are so widespread, such an integral part of your society, you may not recognize that you are in the midst of acting out a behavior-pair. I suggest a review at the end of each day.

Begin With a Blessing

The cleansing process does not take place until you bless it. So, your first step is the prayer of blessing, such as the one that we discussed earlier: "Thank You, God, for Your gifts of body and mind. In Your name, I bless the food, air, and water that sustain me. I bless friends and foes alike, and I resolve that my attitude and actions toward all life be as expansive as Your love for me."

Look for the Sense of Separateness That Defines Fear Behaviors

Now begin to address the behavior-pairs. It is often hard to distinguish well-being from fear when you are immersed in the fear behaviors, because they give you a sense of comfort, a feeling of control of your world. Who is not happy in that situation?

Therein lies the key to identifying fear. If you feel a sense of separateness, of being superior to others in any way, interpret that as a sign that you have crossed the threshold into fear

238

behaviors. You are likely to feel righteous if you are angry or are in the midst of the whirlwind, resolute if you are trying to control another, virtuous if you are acting out the role of the victim or feeling depleted, forward-thinking if you live in the future, and the guardian of a treasure if you live in the past.

All of these feelings—note that they are feelings, not realities—place you in a position of power in relation to your brothers and sisters, not equal to them. Ask yourself this question: *Do I feel the sense of oneness with all life that my blessing signifies?*

Name the Behavior

Often your answer will come, not in the form of a thought but in a feeling. Were you so busy that the day flew by without consideration of anything but work? Did anger at another consume you? Were you depressed and unhappy? Did you worry incessantly about a situation that seems to be getting away from you? Did you spend much of the day dreaming of what you will do five or ten years from now?

This is the point at which you put a name to your behavior: *I lived the day in the whirlwind, and now I'm tired*; or *I am angry with myself for not applying for that new job.*

Deal With the Behavior-Pair

If you are angry with another, or depressed, look below the veil of anger for the change that is bothering you. Then, find out who you blame besides yourself, and forgive her. If you are the target of another's anger, recognize that the other person feels a momentary lightening of her load of fear by directing anger at you. Then, let go of the burden of that anger.

If you are trying to control another, or if you feel like a victim of someone else's control, identify your bottom-line belief. What does someone else owe you? Remember that it is just a belief, a stopping-point on the great circle of duality, not a commandment, and as such is subject to change. Additionally, if you find family and friends distant, and if you limit your own free movement, activities, and thoughts, examine your control issues. You could be immersed in the controlling behavior of withholding, either directly or using the carrot-and-stick approach.

If you are caught in the whirlwind and depletion, or find yourself living in the past and the future, ask what you are running away from in the present.

Silence is key to understanding all your fear behaviors. By incorporating active and reflective silence into each day, you begin to uncover and dismantle them. This is not the time to feel guilty or angry. Look at the day with a sense of detachment, and find the truths hidden in your fear behaviors.

Acknowledge Your Core and Primal Fear-Pairs

Now identify the core fear-pair that most affects you, along with the fear-pairs that hide under it. Additionally, accept the truth that the opposite side of each fear-pair also is part of your worldview. If you fear poverty, what do you fear about abundance? If you fear failure, what do you fear about success? If you fear aging, what do you fear about youth?

Acknowledge the fear of life and death that is buried in these fears. Does poverty lead to death? Does abundance mean death of a type, in that you may have to leave your friends and your way of life?

Uncover and Dismantle the Judgment Under Your Fears

Now, accept that you have made a judgment, and that you believe you are justified in making it. What situation or issue brought up your judgment, and whom do you blame?

Then, dismantle the judgment, by recognizing that the person whom you judge is another human with the same types of hopes and fears that you have, and by accepting that you are attuned to him in some way.

Finally, unveil the desire that lies under your judgment by stating what you would have in this situation, and then let it go. You may have to revisit your decision in time, but there is nothing you can do about it now.

ACCEPTING CHANGE IS KEY

In the end, your key to letting go of fear is accepting change. The more you believe in changelessness—the more you hold on to what you had, rather than accept what you have—the more difficult is your life.

Fear can be a door opener, the key to a treasure. Once you can go past fear to acknowledge the changes that the day brings, you also bring the joys of the present into conscious awareness. You live more authentically and completely.

Honor change, both what you see as positive and what you see as negative, and ask for blessings on all. Then you begin to live with awareness and peace.

EPILOGUE
SETTING UP A CIRCLE OF HAPPINESS

As you step beyond fear,
your heart will open wide.

Guardian of Water Clarification

EPILOGUE:
SETTING UP A CIRCLE OF HAPPINESS

Bow in joy to the miracles that surround you.

Guardian of Water Clarification

Given that we all strive to live in comfort and peace, I asked my devic guides for a prescription for a good life.

* * *

There are two aspects to the prescription that you seek. The first is to walk free from fear—the focus of these communications—and the second is to set up what I term a circle of happiness.

After you make the decision to walk free of fear, you can choose to be happy. I define *happiness* as a state of inner freedom, vitality, and peace. It combines a feeling of contentment with a desire for action, to achieve your life purposes and dreams.

WALK FREE OF FEAR

We begin with fear first. If there is one point that you remember from these discussions, realize that you can never resolve another person's fear.

Fear is an individual choice. If you respond to another's fear or fear behaviors with a judgment or wrong or right, bad or good, you set up a circle of fear that connects you and the other. Beyond that, you frequently expand your circle of fear to include others, often even blaming God, because the first step into fear makes every step that follows easier.

If you would escape your circle of fear, you must accept that the other is experiencing the effects of making a judgment: facing core fears plus the primal fear of life and death, and acting out fear behaviors. Focus on acceptance, on impersonalizing those fear-pairs and fear behaviors as the other's issue, not yours, and you can walk free.

Dealing with your own fear is the only action that you can take. Once you acknowledge the fact that you are fearful, once you bring your judgments, fears, and fear behaviors to light, you begin to experience the loosening of fear's tight grip on your mind and heart.

Let us review the steps that you take to dissolve fear.

If You Find Yourself Uneasy or If You Sense Uneasiness in Another, Accept the Fact That You or the Other Person Are Fearful

You do not have to talk about how fearful you are or act out fear behaviors to have an underlying core of fear, and the same is true of others. You may decide to bottle it inside; however, it is never fully contained.

Common ways that people demonstrate fear are through jerky, nervous movements, particularly of the eyes, head, or hands; a sense of having to rush, even when there is no real need to do so; compulsive behavior, such as eating too much, nail-biting, or other similar mannerisms; a change in the voice, generally toward harshness; a catch in the throat; sweaty forehead or palms; and little or no eye contact. These are precursors to fear behaviors.

Anticipate How You or the Other Will Express Fear

When you see these precursors in yourself or others, ask what your fear behaviors, or those of the other person, are likely to be. The primary ways of imposing fear on others is to blame or shame them, so expect anger plus control as part of the package.

At the same time, are you depressed or feeling like a victim, the shadow side of anger and control? Alternatively, if you are expressing fear but directing it inward, it is likely to show up as the whirlwind, a sense of depletion, or refuge in the past or the future.

The most important aspect of dealing with fear is acceptance, which means that you are not surprised, especially by the fact that you or another are fearful.

Decide to Leave This Atmosphere of Fear

If you are dealing with another person, you can leave the situation by physically walking away from it or calling a time-out. Alternatively, you can mentally accept the fear as the other's issue.

If you are dealing with your own fear, begin to dismantle it piece by piece, as we have discussed: from fear behavior-pair, to core and primal fear-pairs, and finally to the underlying judgment. The key piece in the puzzle is your judgment of bad or good, wrong or right. If you can unlock your judgment, you can walk past fear.

Always keep in mind that there are two great circles in life. The circle of duality has no real stopping point; you simply choose where you will stand, and you accept that others can make different choices. Ask the following questions: *What is my bottom line belief? Is it necessary to impose this belief on others?* When you see it as a belief, not a commandment, you walk toward freedom.

In addition, you have a personal circle, which is constructed differently. Think of it as an endless loop, in which your actions and beliefs circle back to you. It is known in Eastern thought as karma. Keep it as clear as possible, and you walk toward freedom.

CREATE A CIRCLE OF HAPPINESS

You now have a choice to create your personal circle of happiness. I call it a circle, because you reject separation and judgment for union and acceptance each time you enter this circle. You join those who are bringing peace to the Earth, one person at a time.

Begin by Thanking Your Fear and the Fear That Surrounds You

You enter your circle of happiness by accepting and thanking your fear. Fear is a big part of most people's lives, with up to seventy-five percent of their waking hours spent in fear, but those hours are a gift. Only through the absence of love—in other words, through fear—can you recognize the fullness and beauty of love. Fear is a step on your pathway to wholeness.

Bless All Every Day

Continue with a prayer of blessing, such as the one we have used in these discussions: "Thank You, God, for Your gifts of body and mind. In Your name, I thank and bless the food, air, and water that sustain me. I bless friends and foes alike, and I resolve that my attitude and actions toward all life be as expansive as Your love for me."

People often believe that they must use dissatisfaction or unhappiness as a catalyst to a better life, but it does not work that way. You grow from the happiness that you have at present to expanded happiness. In your blessing, you acknowledge happiness as your baseline.

Honor Your Body

What are your eating habits? How much time do you set aside for exercise, preferably outdoors? Keep your body in peak condition, so you will have the energy and vitality to pursue your dreams, as well as enjoy life day-to-day.

Call on Your Body to Teach Your Mind

As the Guardian of Communication has advised, smile. The mind looks to the body for wisdom that can only be tapped physically. In time, your mind will learn to read your smile as an indicator that you can live in inner joy, even if fears assail you.

Remember also that most fears either dissipate before they become reality, or they manifest in a different way from that which you anticipate.

Set Aside Time for Active and Reflective Silence Every Day

Silence is essential. If you have the acclaim of many for your good deeds and works, yet do not feel a sense of completion, what is your reward? Is the praise of others more important than your own inner sense of satisfaction?

Set aside at least fifteen minutes for active silence each day—time in nature, exercise, cooking, woodworking, and the like—with your goal breadth of spirit. Additionally, reserve at least fifteen minutes for reflective silence—poetry, religious texts, prayer, or meditation—to expand your mind beyond the movement and noise of everyday life.

Plan to use active and reflective silence throughout your life. They are vital for your physical and mental health.

Take Time for Expansion

If you have something undone in your life, do it. Additionally, take time each day to admire something you usually take for granted: a lovely stone, a flower, the smile on your child's face. There are wonders all around you. Preferably, do this outdoors. You need to spend time in a place that is bigger than the confines of your manmade world.

These actions force you into the present, and because they do so, they are your keys to happiness. Joy is now, this moment; it is never found yesterday or tomorrow.

EXPANSION IS KEY TO HEALING OURSELVES AND THE PLANET

There is an expanded world waiting for you. The pot of gold at the end of the rainbow may not be real, but the riches at the end of your journey through fear are beyond measure.

These gifts are hinted at by quantum physics: You can think your world whole. Picture the most wonderful treasures imaginable, including miracles of healing, peace on Earth, and revitalization of the planet's eco-climate. Beyond that, picture instantaneous travel to far reaches of the universe, and dialogues with life forms from

251

other planets and planes. Our thought, and yours, can create those kinds of miracles.

In truth, you can expand to wherever your mind would take you, once you grow past fear to love. Earlier we said that only ten percent of humanity has to learn to think outside the fear-box in order to begin to effect planetary transformation. Take the first step on your journey through fear, and you not only help yourself; you take the first step toward bringing about changes more immense than you can imagine.

ADDITIONAL READING

Altman, Nathaniel. *The Deva Handbook.* Rochester, Vermont: Destiny Books, 1995.

Bonnett, O. T., M.D. *Why Healing Happens.* Huntsville, Arkansas: Ozark Mountain Publishing, 2006.

Boone, J. Allen. *Kinship with All Life.* New York: Harper & Row Publishers, 1954.

Cowan, Eliot. *Plant Spirit Medicine.* Newberg, Oregon: Swan-Raven & Company, 1995.

Findhorn Community. *The Findhorn Garden.* New York: Harper & Row Publishers, 1975.

Fraser, Gwennie Armstrong. *The Golden Web: A New Partnership with Nature.* Scotland: Findhorn Press, 1995.

Goldsmith, Joel S. *Consciousness Unfolding.* Lakewood, Colorado: Acropolis Books, Inc., 1999.

Maclean, Dorothy. *To Hear the Angels Sing.* Hudson, New York: Lindisfarne Press, 1990.

Penčzak, Christopher. *Spirit Allies: Meet Your Team from the Other Side.* San Francisco, CA: Weiser Books, 2002.

Pogačnik, Marko. *Nature Spirits and Elemental Beings: Working with the Intelligence in Nature.* Scotland, Findhorn Press, 1995.

Roads, Michael J. *Talking With Nature.* Tiburon, CA: HJ Kramer, Inc., 1987.

_____. *Journey Into Nature: A Spiritual Adventure.* Tiburon, CA: HJ Kramer, Inc., 1990.

_____. *Journey Into Oneness: A Spiritual Odyssey.* Tiburon, CA: HJ Kramer, Inc., 1994.

Roberts, Jane, and Robert F. Butts. *Adventures in Consciousness: An Introduction to Aspect Psychology.* Needham, MA: Moment Point Press, 1999.

Talbot, Michael. *The Holographic Universe.* New York: Harper Collins, 1992.

Tolle, Eckhart. *A New Earth: Awakening to Your Life's Purpose.* New York: Dutton, 2005.

_____. *The Power of Now: A Guide to Spiritual Enlightenment.* Novato, California: New World Library, 1999.

Tompkins, Peter. *The Secret Life of Nature.* New York: HarperCollins Publishers, 1997.

_____ and Christopher Bird. *The Secret Life of Plants.* New York: Harper & Row Publishers, 1973.

VanGelder, Dora. *The Real World of Fairies.* Wheaton, Illinois: The Theosophical Publishing House, 1977.

Wright, Machaelle Small. *Perelandra Garden Workbook, Second Edition: A Complete Guide to Gardening with Nature Intelligences.* Warrenton, Virginia: Perelandra, Ltd., 1993.

Yogananda, Paramahansa. *Autobiography of a Yogi.* Los Angeles: Self Realization Fellowship, 2006.

About the Author

Antoinette Lee Howard

As a child growing up in the Northeast, Antoinette knew she was a writer and artist, with a life at Walden Pond her dream. She received her M.A. in Professional Writing from the University of Southern California, but she chose a less traditional path in art, with college classes for the basics, followed by four years of intensive study with abstract painter Aidron Duckworth. She now calls the Southwest home.

It was not until she decided to shift her love for writing and illustration from computer training and grant proposals to the natural world—her version of that early dream—that she became aware of devic presences. *Journey Through Fear* is the result of six years of communications with these guardians.

The theme that emerges from these messages is that we live in a field of unity, which includes everything we see, everything we touch, and ultimately everything we *are*. However, we block this truth with fear, which locks us into the belief that we are disconnected and alone.

For most of us, fear thought-structures occupy seventy-five percent of our waking hours. *Journey Through Fear* offers a way to dismantle them, with peace individually, and in time worldwide, our priceless gift for doing so.

You may email Antoinette at devicmessages@yahoo.com

Other Books Published
by
Ozark Mountain Publishing, Inc.

Conversations with Nostradamus, Volume I, II, III.................by Dolores Cannon
Jesus and the Essenes..by Dolores Cannon
They Walked with Jesus..by Dolores Cannon
Between Death and Life.. by Dolores Cannon
A Soul Remembers Hiroshima...by Dolores Cannon
Keepers of the Garden..by Dolores Cannon
The Legend of Starcrash..by Dolores Cannon
The Custodians..by Dolores Cannon
The Convoluted Universe - Book One, Two, Three..............by Dolores Cannon
I Have Lived Before...by Sture Lönnerstrand
The Forgotten Woman...by Arun & Sunanda Gandhi
Luck Doesn't Happen by Chance..................................by Claire Doyle Beland
Mankind - Child of the Stars............................by Max H. Flindt & Otto Binder
The Gnostic Papers..by John V. Panella
Past Life Memories As A Confederate Soldier.......................by James H. Kent
Holiday in Heaven...by Aron Abrahamsen
Is Jehovah An E.T.?...by Dorothy Leon
The Ultimate Dictionary of Dream Language.........................by Briceida Ryan
The Essenes - Children of the Light..............by Stuart Wilson & Joanna Prentis
Power of the Magdalene..............................by Stuart Wilson & Joanna Prentis
Rebirth of the Oracle..................................by Justine Alessi & M. E. McMillan
Reincarnation: The View from Eternity......by O.T. Bonnett, M.D. & Greg Satre
The Divinity Factor..by Donald L. Hicks
What I Learned After Medical School ....by O.T. Bonnett, M.D.
Why Healing Happens..by O.T. Bonnett, M.D.
A Journey Into Being...by Christine Ramos, RN
Discover The Universe Within You..by Mary Letorney
Worlds Beyond Death..by Rev. Grant H. Pealer
Let's Get Natural With Herbs..by Debra Rayburn
The Enchanted Garden..by Jodi Felice
My Teachers Wear Fur Coats.......................by Susan Mack & Natalia Krawetz
Seeing True...by Ronald Chapman
Elder Gods of Antiquity...by M. Don Schorn
Legacy of the Elder Gods...by M. Don Schorn

Continue for more books by Ozark Mountain Publishing, Inc.

Children of the Stars .... by Nikki Pattillo
Angels - The Guardians of Your Destiny ....by Maiya & Geoff Gray-Cobb
Seeds of the Soul..by Maiya Gray-Cobb
The Despiritualized Church...by Rev. Keith Bender
The Science of Knowledge ....by Vara Humphreys
The Other Side of Suicide ....by Karen Peebles
Journey Through Fear ....by Antoinette Lee Howard
Awakening To Your Creation ....by Julia Hanson

For more information about any of the above titles, soon to be released titles, or other items in our catalog, write or visit our website:

OZARK
MOUNTAIN
PUBLISHING

PO Box 754
Huntsville, AR 72740
www.ozarkmt.com
1-800-935-0045/479-738-2348
Wholesale Inquiries Welcome